RUGBY FOR BEGINNERS

My demonstrators—Kevin, David and Douglas.

RUGBY FOR BEGINNERS

RAY WILLIAMS

Welsh Rugby Union
Coaching Organiser

SOUVENIR PRESS

First published 1973 by Souvenir Press Ltd,
95 Mortimer Street, London W1N 8HP
and simultaneously in Canada by
J. M. Dent & Sons (Canada) Ltd,
Ontario, Canada
Reprinted January 1974
Reprinted July 1974

ISBN 0 285 62093 2

Filmset in Photon Times 12 on 14 pt. by
Richard Clay (The Chaucer Press), Ltd, Bungay, Suffolk
Printed in Great Britain by
Fletcher & Son Ltd, Norwich

CONTENTS

To

MEGAN, JUDITH and HELEN

for, by their sacrifice and understanding they, too, have
made a particular contribution to the Game.

AUTHOR'S NOTE

This book is, in particular, aimed at the young beginner but
it will also be of great value to those who teach and coach
the young. Many books by distinguished authors have been
written on this theme but I have tried to present the new
thinking which has characterised Rugby Football in recent
years. Whether I have succeeded or not is not for me to
judge.

Whatever the final assessment is I must thank Mr Cliff
Jones, a great Welsh outside-half of the pre-war era and still
an indefatigable worker for the game, for his generous
Foreword; Peter Oatley Swain for his excellent line-
drawings; Mrs Carole Tucker and Mrs Marion Florance
who typed the script and finally, but certainly not least,
David, Douglas and Kevin, my demonstrators, who by their
skill show that they have a future in the game.

The rest, including the photographs, is my responsibility
alone. I hope my efforts have not been in vain.

RAY WILLIAMS

FOREWORD

By CLIFF JONES

(*Chairman of the Welsh Rugby Union Coaching Committee*)

Any attacking fly-half playing pre-war, as I did, was hampered by laws which favoured the defenders, particularly those destructive wing forwards who thrived on the prevailing conditions.

It is, therefore, most gratifying to be honoured with the writing of this foreword at a time when Rugby Football has taken on a new lease of life.

This upsurge in the game, beneficial to both players and spectators alike, was a result of two important developments. First, the skilful changes in the laws introduced by the International Board, which successfully curbed the activities of the spoilers from set pieces and created more room for attackers to manoeuvre, and secondly, the advent and the acceptance of COACHING at all levels of the game. Through coaching the old negative defensive attitude which prevailed for so long from the 1920s to the 1960s was thrown completely overboard. In its place came a new *positive* approach —that of aggressive attacking *team* play with the 4 pt. try-line as the be-all and end-all of its existence.

It follows from this positive approach that "POSSESSION" is a first priority and that all players must be "ball-getters". From "POSSESSION" through good scrummaging, line-out and broken play, will flow the fundamentals of *team* play (which have never really changed since the game began). These fundamental principles are so important as to warrant repetition even in a foreword. They are:

(1) Go FORWARD.

(2) Support, support, support and

(3) Continuity until the line is crossed.

Lastly if "POSSESSION" is lost, then you must put your opponents under extreme "pressure", relentless and constant as we have so often witnessed from "All Blacks" teams in their long and glorious history.

These, then, are the solid foundations upon which Mr Ray Williams has based his coaching methods in this book, coupled with a new and absorbing chapter on "Mini-Rugby", an excellent means of introducing the game to the *very* young.

To reduce the complexities of the game to simplicities is the aim of a *good* coach and all who have come under the Author's influence will testify as to his exceptional ability in this respect. Having been actively involved in Rugby football for over forty years, I believe this book to be a most worth-while contribution towards the improvement of any player's game and every player's enjoyment.

CLIFF JONES

1   INTRODUCTION

So you want to be a Rugby player. The chances are that you want to be a *good* Rugby player, that you have visions of being the greatest. If you are English, Scottish or Irish you will dream of playing at Twickenham, Murrayfield or Lansdowne Road, while if you are Welsh your dreams will be filled with John Williams, Gerald Davies, Barry John and Gareth Edwards. You will be wearing the red jersey and running on to that great stadium at the Cardiff Arms Park, now with its huge new North Stand, modern and with it, but the ghosts of the great players of the past are still there lurking in the background.

We, all of us, whatever our particular interest, owe a great deal to the past. For it is from the deeds of those who went before us that we find the inspiration which enables us to pursue and enjoy a particular activity. Rugby football owes much to the past and especially to a young Englishman, William Webb Ellis, who, in 1823, introduced a new dimension into football, that of running with the ball. His deed is commemorated in a plaque in the grounds of Rugby School where he was a sixteen-year-old pupil at the time. The inscription on the plaque says:

THIS STONE
COMMEMORATES THE EXPLOIT OF
WILLIAM WEBB ELLIS
WHO, WITH A FINE DISREGARD FOR THE RULES OF FOOTBALL
AS PLAYED IN HIS TIME,
FIRST TOOK THE BALL IN HIS ARMS AND RAN WITH IT
THUS ORIGINATING THE DISTINCTIVE FEATURE OF
THE RUGBY GAME
A.D. 1823

There is often a great deal of misunderstanding concerning the football that was played at that particular time. There were numerous forms of the game. Nearly all of them allowed handling and kicking. The accepted method was to catch the ball, kick and chase it. No one, apparently, had thought of catching the ball and running with it. In the same way, no one thought of dribbling with the feet. Eventually these two distinctive features did emerge and laid the foundations for the two great football codes—Rugby and Association.

In recent years many Rugby historians have questioned whether William Webb Ellis really was the boy who started it all. The history of the early game is not well-recorded and therefore there is some doubt about the truth of the William Webb Ellis story. However, the legend has grown and is part of the Rugby folk-lore; it appeals to the romantics and I, for one, would feel cheated and disappointed if someone was able to prove to me that William Webb Ellis did not start Rugby football as we know it. It will be rather like the situation which would have arisen in 1905 if R. G. Deans of New Zealand *had* scored a try against Wales at the Cardiff Arms Park in that historic game which Wales won by 3 points to nil. For those of you who do not know the events surrounding the game, here is a brief resumé.

The year was 1905 and the New Zealand National side, the All Blacks, were undertaking their first tour of Great Britain and Europe. They had swept all before them, except in Wales, where then, as now, the standard was especially high. The highlight of the tour was the international against Wales. In a closely fought game against the unbeaten All Blacks, Wales were leading by a try (3 points then) to nothing. Suddenly there was a New Zealand attack and R. G. Deans was tackled just short of the line. At least he says that he crossed the line but that, by the time the referee arrived, the Welshmen had pulled him back into the field of play.

"No try," said the referee and Wales won. However the referee's decision sparked off a great controversy which has raged over the years. Deans, reputedly, said on his deathbed that he did score a try against Wales and even now New Zealanders visit the Cardiff Arms Park to look at the spot where he said it occurred. My own view is that if he had scored, the game would be that much poorer because the incident established a great and lasting bond between the Rugby men of Wales and New Zealand. In the same way I prefer to believe that it was William Webb Ellis who, with a brilliant piece of initiative, ran with the ball and, at one fell swoop, created Rugby football.

We have, of course, got two kinds of Rugby—the Union game and the League game. This arose quite early in the development of Rugby football. A group of clubs in the North of England decided that players who lost wages through playing should be recompensed. This was a view which was not shared by the vast majority of Rugby people in Britain at that time. The result was the formation of the Northern Union which eventually became the Rugby Football League. This split took place in 1893 and the objections to "broken-time payments", as they were called, because it was felt that they were the fore-runners of a professional game, were fully justified. Rugby League, as we all know, is now played professionally. As far as Great Britain is concerned, it is confined almost entirely to Yorkshire and Lancashire.

Rugby Union Football on the other hand is a completely amateur game. Apart from the small staff employed by each governing body to assist in the promotion and development of the game, no one gets paid for taking part in the game. The first governing body to be formed to control the game was the Rugby Football Union founded in 1871. It is interesting to note that it is not prefaced by the word "English", for it was the only one in the World at that particular time.

This distinctive title is very jealously guarded by members of the Rugby Football Union who recently celebrated the centenary of the formation of the Union. Part of the centenary celebrations was the organising of a Congress to study the development and future enjoyment of the game. Such is the growth of Rugby that at this Congress there were representatives from fifty Rugby playing nations from all parts of the World.

The formation of the Rugby Football Union in 1871 was followed by that of the Scottish Rugby Union in 1872; the Irish Rugby Union in 1879 and the Welsh Rugby Union in 1880. The supreme governing body in Rugby Union Football is the International Rugby Football Board and this is composed of England, Scotland, Ireland, Wales, New Zealand, Australia and South Africa. This is the body which produces the laws of the game and in fact it lays down the policy for the general conduct and development of the game.

2 PRINCIPLES OF PLAY

So much then for a very brief historical background to the game. You will be more interested in playing it and in knowing how you can learn the game most effectively.

If you are a beginner to the game it is far better to begin simply for the complete game is fairly complicated. This is one reason, why, for players under twelve years, I think that Mini-Rugby (described elsewhere) is such a good introduction.

Where then, do we begin? For instance how important are the Laws of the Game? There are certainly a lot of them, twenty-seven to be precise. However I do not want you to be too concerned with the laws for these you will learn as you get more experience. I do, however, want to introduce you to one law. This is Law 7 entitled Mode of Play. It tells you what you can do, whereas all the other laws, in a sense, tell you what you cannot do.

Law 7. Mode of Play
A match is started by a kick-off, after which any player who is on-side may at any time:

- catch or pick up the ball and run with it,
- pass, throw or knock the ball to another player,
- kick or otherwise propel the ball,
- tackle, push or shoulder an opponent holding the ball,
- fall on the ball,
- take part in scrummage, ruck, maul or line-out provided he does so in accordance with these Laws.

If we ignore the last paragraph for the moment, we can see that all players, if they are on-side, can catch the ball, pick it up and run with it. They can pass or throw it; they can kick it. They can tackle an opponent holding the ball and they can fall on the ball. All these things which a player can do can be summed up as basic individual skills. These are the Rugby footballer's alphabet and until you have acquired them you will not be able to express yourself fluently in the game. When you are learning another language, you may be engaged in a simple conversation and suddenly you come to a word which you cannot pronounce or do not know. This obviously limits what you can say. So it is with Rugby, if all the skills are not at your command this limits your game and consequently the game of your team.

My next point is that Rugby football is a team game. It is about players co-operating with each other so that they can more effectively try to beat their opponents. This matter of co-operation however does not just happen, we have to work at it. It is perfectly possible for fifteen individuals to play in a team but not *as* a team. If each player plays for himself, then the chances are that the team will not play as well as it might. I am going to suggest, therefore, that, although you have, first of all, to learn your Rugby alphabet, which, in its absolutely simplest form is handling, running, tackling and kicking, you must realise that these skills are only a means to an end. In this case the end is playing as a team.

Before we can decide to play as a team we have to know what is involved. We have to understand the principles of team play and, until we do, being able to pass, kick, run and tackle will not really mean anything. There are four principles of team play, they are:

1. Go forward
2. Support
3. Continuity
4. Pressure

Let us look at them in closer detail.

1. Go forward

This is something that the whole team must be prepared to do. Trying to play the game going backwards or sideways is making it much more difficult. Yet, if you were to watch many teams you would see that there is little emphasis on going forward. We must also remember that unless you do go forward at some stage you can never score a try.

2. Support

Have you ever thought how long a player actually has the ball in his possession during the course of a game? I have heard all sorts of answers ranging from four minutes to eleven minutes. Therefore I am sure you will be surprised when I tell you that no player, even in a senior game, has the ball in his hands throughout the whole game for longer than one minute; one minute in eighty. If this is the case, we now come to the 64,000-dollar question. What does he do during the other seventy-nine minutes? The answer is that he supports the ball. All players must learn to run off the ball. This is not merely a matter of running blindly, and anywhere, but it involves thought and anticipation so that a player can make the right decision in terms of where and how he should run.

3. Continuity

If we are going forward and we have got support we must obviously keep the game going because the other side are in trouble. The dropped pass, the poor kick, the collapsed ruck usually causes the game to be stopped and often the ball is given to the opposition. So not only are the opponents relieved of their troubles but they are also given possession. We must therefore practice our continuity techniques— handling, kicking, rucking, mauling are all means by which we can keep the game going.

4. Pressure

Having the ball unfortunately is only about 50 per cent
of the game. In normal circumstances we can say that the
opposition will have the ball during a game for about as long
as we have it. What do we do about it? We take the game to
them; we deny them time and space. In other words we put
them under pressure. It is pressure that causes the opposition to make mistakes and opposition mistakes give us the
opportunity to regain possession.

This then is the basic background to the team game and
we must remember that the only reason for improving our
handling, running, tackling and kicking is that we are more
able to go forward, to support the ball, to maintain continuity and, when the other side have the ball, to put them
under pressure.

3 INDIVIDUAL SKILL

Not so long ago those who taught others to play Rugby football did it by teaching players to pass, to tackle and so on. More often than not those being taught had very few ideas on even how the game was played. I am glad to say that this has gradually changed. For example if you have read the preceding chapter carefully you will know what the principles of team play are. If you do not know, then go back and read that chapter again!

There is now much more emphasis in teaching and coaching on the skill aspect. Previously we assumed that teaching someone to pass, kick and tackle was the same as teaching them to play the game. This is not so. Let me explain why. If I were to give you a ball and tell you to pass it to me, you would, I am sure, do it reasonably well and perhaps with more practice and little help from me you would do it very well. You would have developed a good TECHNIQUE. However, the techniques of most Rugby skills are relatively simple. It is having to do them when other people are trying to stop you that makes them more difficult. Although you may have acquired good passing technique by practising with me, the chances are that if you were put into a Rugby game without any further experience your passing technique would not be so good. This is because of the factors which are now acting against you, such as the speed with which things are happening, the opposition trying to prevent you from making a good pass and your own team-mates who perhaps are not being as helpful as they might! In fact being able to perform technique in the game is what we call SKILL. Nowadays coaches try to make the teaching of techniques as realistic as possible. They try to get them as near to the game situation as they can. They put the technique under pressure because this is what you will have to cope with in the game.

You, yourself, can help to acquire skill when playing small games with and against other players. One very simple illustration is a passing game played in a 10-yard square two players against two others. One pair starts off with the ball and they see how many passes they can make before they drop it or before the opponents intercept it. There is no tackling, passes can be made in any direction but no player is allowed outside the area. If this happens or the ball is dropped or a pass intercepted, then the ball goes to the opposition. By playing this kind of game players learn to make decisions; they learn to "support" the ball; they practise their "continuity" techniques and they also learn to put "pressure" on the opposition. These, as we know, are all principles of team play.

In adopting this approach you will shorten the learning process but, more than this, practice will never become boring because of the infinite variety in it. The enjoyment factor will be very high and therefore you will be prepared to work harder and longer. You are, in fact, even in a two-a-side game playing a form of Rugby football, you are involved in competition and therefore there is a real chance that the ability which you show in terms of technique and in the making and taking of decisions will transfer to the big game. In essence what I am saying is that learning *when* to do something in a game is as important if not more important as learning *how*.

The chapters which follow will be concerned for the most part with "how" but there is a lot of space later on devoted to "when". Before dealing about technique in detail, I think it is important for you to understand that there is no one way. You will, with experience, develop your own, but you have to start somewhere and I am going to suggest some fundamental principles which you should try to follow. Coaches in the past have laid a great deal of stress on style—on what a player looked like before, during or after he had passed the ball. The most important thing about any pass is that it should be easy for the receiver to take and what happens to the ball should be the main consideration. What the passer looks like is really immaterial. Similarly, when a player kicks for goal, the really important thing is whether it goes over. If it does, it is a good kick. Again we have to start somewhere and there are some basic principles which will help those whose kicking experience is very limited. It may be, too, that a poor kicker is unsuccessful because the technique is poor and here attention to basic principles may well help. It is with these thoughts in mind that I want you to read the remainder of this book.

4 HANDLING

I have deliberately entitled this chapter "Handling" although many people might prefer to call it "Passing". I think my term is the better one because not only does it cover passing and all kinds of passes at that, it also covers receiving the ball, from pass or kick, picking up the ball, even falling on the ball. Perhaps I should also say that I try to keep my advice simple so that you will not be confused and therefore I draw attention to what I consider to be the KEY FACTORS. If you follow these I am confident you will not go far wrong.

The first key factor when running with the ball is to carry it in two hands. This means that you are always in a position to pass it. The ball tucked under one arm is a "dead" ball. You can do nothing with it. I have seen many players who have developed the habit—a bad one—of always tucking the ball under one arm. It has become an automatic action and the player is less effective as a result. If a player runs with the ball in two hands the defender has to be concerned with three things, the ball, the ball-carrier and the support. The player who tucks the ball makes it easy for the defender because as the ball is "dead" he cannot pass it, therefore the defender does not have to worry about the support. He can concentrate his efforts on the ball-carrier. Carry the ball in two hands is therefore sound advice, practise it. Tucking is permissible, indeed it is necessary, when you want to hand-off an opponent but do remember to tuck the ball under the arm further away from the defender so that the nearer arm can be used for the hand-off.

Another general principle in handling is that you should

Fig. 1. Try to take the ball early whether from a pass . . .

Fig. 2. . . . or a kick.

try to take the ball early whether from a pass or a kick. (Figs 1 and 2.) When you take the ball early from a pass, by reaching for it, it means that you can pass the ball on, if you wish to, very quickly. Try to avoid pulling the ball into the body, this only slows down the pass and destroys the passing rhythm. Keep the ball away from the body at all times. You may have to break this rule when, perhaps the ball is very wet, but techniques, of course, must always be adapted to suit particular conditions. One word, too, about the actual technique of receiving the ball. The arms are reaching for the ball but they are not rigid and when the ball makes contact with the hands they give slightly and act as shock-absorbers. The ball, too, is caught with the fingers because this is where we have the greatest amount of control.

From a kick the same general principles apply. Reach for the ball, catch it in the fingers but, this time because the force will be much greater, it is necessary to pull the ball into the body. I must emphasise however that the ball must be taken in the fingers and then brought into the "basket" formed by the hands, arms and chest. This time the knees and body give and so act as shock-absorbers. It is also good practice as the ball is being caught to turn slightly to one side so as to prevent the possibility of a knock-on and also to produce a strong position in order to resist a tackle.

Let us now consider the various methods of passing the ball:

THE BASIC PASS

This is the pass that most of us associate with Rugby. It is the pass which is given to a player who is running in support of the ball-carrier, alongside him and about 5 yards away. You must remember that the main aim is to make it an easy pass to take, BUT, in addition, it must also be an easy pass to transfer onwards.

Key factors

1. Look at the player to whom you are going to pass
2. Ball in two hands
3. Swing the ball
4. Keep the ball stable in the air
5. Pass in front of the receiver

These points need some further explanation.

Look at the receiver   This really is most important because
this will be the first indication to the supporting player that
you are going to pass to him and it allows him to prepare to
receive the ball. It is still perfectly possible to see the defenders out of the corner of your eye. This is what we call
peripheral vision, you need not remember the name but you
must remember what it means. Rugby would be a very
difficult game if you had to play it with horse blinkers on,
because you could not see what was happening around you.
Therefore you try to take in as much as you can see.

Ball in two hands   This point has already been made, but it
is much safer to use two hands. However, it must be said
that it is quite acceptable to pass the ball with one hand
sometimes indeed it may be the only way you can get the
ball away. However, it should be regarded as the exception
rather than the rule and perhaps is best left to more experienced players.

Swing the ball   This is the basic element of technique.
Swinging the ball does two things, it is a further indication
(looking is the first) to the receiver that the pass is to be
made and it provides the necessary impetus to the pass to
enable it to reach the receiver. The passer who "flicks" the
ball with his wrists often takes the receiver by surprise. So
much so on some occasions that he snatches at the ball and
sometimes drops it. The "flick" pass, too, often has not got

the strength to reach the receiver and it dips, again causing him sometimes to miss it.

Keep the ball stable   Obviously a ball that "sits" up in the air is so much easier to take than one which is turning over and over. It really is a matter of correct hold on the ball. You can achieve this quite simply; hold the ball out in front of you, elbows into the side, your hands should now be underneath the ball with the little fingers almost touching. When you look at your hands you will only be able to see your thumbs. This will ensure that when you pass the ball your hands are behind it. The tips of the fingers are in the centre of the ball, if they were nearer the top or the bottom they would cause the ball to wobble in flight. (Figs 3 and 4.)

Pass in front   Every player who passes a ball should never be satisfied with less than perfection. As far as the receiver is concerned this is a pass which comes at the right speed—easy to take—at the right height—level with his hips—and in front of him. The target area therefore is small and there is little margin for error. When I tell you that players of the calibre of John Dawes, Barry John, Arthur Lewis and Gareth Edwards spend their time in practise concentrating on hitting the target area you will appreciate how important it is and even they do not always succeed. When you practise you ought to be aiming for the target area and remember it is not sufficient for the receiver merely to have caught the ball. The ball must have been at the right speed, at the right height and in front of the receiver—the perfect pass.

THE SCREEN PASS

The name of this pass is an indication of the kind of pass that it is. The ball-carrier screens or protects the ball from the opposition. It is a pass which, in particular, is used by forwards but all players should be able to use it when the

Fig. 3. This is the way to hold the ball . . .

Fig. 4. . . . so that when it is passed it "sits up" in the air.

circumstances call for it. It is best used when there are a number of players in a confined area. The emphasis is on driving forward with support. In one sense it is not a pass at all because the ball-carrier offers the ball and the supporting player takes it out of his hands. It also has the effect of committing the opposition and, as a result, of creating space.

Key factors

1. Drive forward at the opposition
2. Screen the ball
3. Support

Let us analyse these points.

1. *Drive forward* The emphasis here must be on using a shoulder. You drive into the opposition by dropping your shoulder. The All Blacks lay great stress on this for all forwards as a prelude to rucking. Some New Zealand coaches in criticising their own players during the 1971 Lions tour said that New Zealand players went into rucks too upright. The matter of body position is important because a low body position achieved by dropping a shoulder is a strong position and is what we want in the screen pass. The object should be to keep driving—through the opposition if possible. Many people in coaching this pass teach turning the back on the opponent. In fact I did it myself at one period, I now believe the driving shoulder method to be more effective. You might knock your opponent over in which case you are still in a forward running position.

2. *Screen the ball* If you are going to be in physical contact with the opposition it does mean that the ball is vulnerable. There is nothing worse than to see a player making a dynamic surge forward only to see an opponent taking the ball from him. All players must learn to protect possession, for possession belongs not to an individual but to the team.

Fig. 5. The screen pass—a good example of protecting possession.

Fig. 6. See how the supporter has come in close in order to take the ball. The low driving position of the supporter is a strong position. Perhaps he could be even lower.

In order to do this the player when he drops his shoulder to make contact must push the ball back to his opposite hip. Let us say that he drives with his right shoulder at an opponent he must then push the ball back in both hands to his left hip. Note I state in *both* hands I do not believe as some people do that the ball should be held against the hip by one hand. You have much more control with two hands. (Fig. 5.)

3. *Support*   The success of this kind of pass is entirely dependent on really close support, for the supporter must take the ball out of the ball-carrier's hands. There is too a special technique for the supporter. He must also drop his shoulder as he goes to take the ball. This will ensure that he is in a powerful driving position and so will be very difficult to stop. (Fig. 6.)

SWITCH PASS

A method of changing the direction of attack. It is especially useful near the touch-lines when space is limited. It can be used as a move by three-quarters, usually between the centres, and a dummy switch can also be used, i.e. pretending to switch pass but although both the ball-carrier and the potential receiver run, the ball is not transferred. It is surprising how successful this move can be.

Key factors

    1. The ball-carrier must widen the angle
    2. Screen the ball
    3. Support

Again let us analyse the points.

1. *Ball-carrier*   He must widen the angle of his run. In other words he must run across the path of the receiver. The effect of this will be to take the opposition with him and so

widen the gap for the receiver to run through. The ball-carrier has created space. Imagine two players running parallel to the touch-line and about 5 yards apart. The inside man, who has the ball, starts the switch by suddenly swinging out towards his partner, he runs across his partner's path, who comes in close and takes the ball from the ball-carrier's hands. The attack has now been switched to a different line. (Fig. 7.)

2. Screen the ball   This is done differently from the method previously outlined in the screen pass. Here the ball-carrier turns towards the receiver and offers him the ball. It means that the defence lose sight of the ball and it is this fact which makes the dummy so successful. Turning towards the receiver also means that the ball-carrier can see him and that the receiver can see the ball.

3. Support   As in the screen pass this must be very close. I always recommend that the receiver takes the ball out of the ball-carrier's hands. In this way there is little chance of the ball being dropped as the result of a poor pass. (Fig. 8.)

The next group of passes are really the particular ones required by the scrum-half, although all players must be familiar with them. There may well be a maul in which the scrum-half is caught and it is obviously necessary for someone to take his place. The someone could be a prop forward but at that moment in time he is a scrum-half, a very good reason why he should be able to get the ball away quickly and effectively.

A relatively recent innovation in scrum-half passes has been the development of the spin pass. It was first done consistently well in this country by Chris Laidlaw when he came with the 1967 All Blacks. This technique, however, was adopted by Gareth Edwards who now is regarded as possibly the longest server of a ball in Rugby history. This great length is undoubtedly the result of spinning the ball so

Fig. 7. The switch pass—widen the angle by running across the path of the receiver. *Hand* the ball to him.

Fig. 8. The pass has been completed and the attack switched to a different line.

that it travels through the air like a bullet does when it leaves a gun. In this way the ball offers much less resistance to the air and it obviously goes further. It is a very important technique in the scrum-half's armoury and needs to be developed at an early age.

However, the spin pass should, in my opinion, only be used when extra length is required. I often see three-quarters spin-passing in a normal back-line. This is both unnecessary and dangerous, unnecessary because the orthodox pass is perfectly adequate and dangerous because the spinning ball is more difficult to take. You may say that if it is dangerous why bother to use it at all. I think the extra length which you get by using the spin pass from the scrum-half position more than justifies the risk element there is in receiving it but in the three-quarter situation there is no need to hazard the pass in this way.

How then does one produce a spin pass? We know, because I have described it earlier, that in the orthodox pass, the ball is held along its length, i.e. with the fingers running parallel to the seams. In order to spin pass the ball it must be held so that the fingers run at right angles to the seams. (Fig. 12.) The spinning technique is easy to learn. Hold the ball with both hands, arms straight out in front of you at shoulder height. If your fingers are across the seams the ball will be "standing up" straight. If you are right-handed swing the ball to the left, letting it roll off the tips of the fingers as it leaves your right hand, vice versa if you are left-handed. The ball will now spin through the air rather like a top. Of course you cannot pass it in a game like this because in this position it offers a lot of resistance to the wind. At least however, you can make it spin and by reproducing that movement in a different plane you can get the ball to spin point first and get greater length.

This is quite easy to achieve, hold the ball again but instead of holding it at shoulder height let the arms hang naturally and point the ball in the direction you want it to go. Swing the ball in a passing movement to the left (right-handed players) and roll the ball off the tips of the fingers of the right hand. The ball should spin point first. If it does not, keep practising, it soon will. The spin pass is almost solely a one-handed pass. This is why some players can only spin pass well to one side. The players who hope to be good must practise very hard with their "poor" hand in order to improve it.

In the techniques of scrum-half passing which I now describe either the spin pass or the orthodox pass can be used.

STRAIGHT PASS

This is the easiest pass for the scrum-half because it does not involve any turning and he can see the player to whom he is trying to pass all the time. The object is to get the ball as quickly as possible from the ground or from the hands, if it is passed directly to the scrum-half from a line-out or maul, to the receiver.

Key factors
1. Back foot close to ball
2. Wide base
3. Sweep the ball away

1. *Back foot*   There are two main reasons why the back foot should be close to the ball. The first is that by doing so the ball is protected and less liable to interference. The second, and more important, is that from this position the ball can be swept away without any wind-up. (Fig. 9.)

2. *Wide base*   The front foot must be pushed out towards the receiver, this gives a firm and wide base which will enable the passer to accelerate the ball in order to give a long pass. (Figs 10 and 13.)

Fig. 9. The orthodox straight pass from the ground. See how close the back foot is to the ball.

Fig. 10. See how the weight is transferred on a wide base from back to front foot. Compare the handhold on the ball with that in Fig. 13.

Fig. 11. The ball is swept away and the pass completed.

Fig. 12. The handhold necessary in order to spin pass the ball.

Fig. 13. The straight spin pass, all the other principles are the same, but the handhold is different—compare with Fig. 10.

Fig. 14. The spin pass completed. One hand is always dominant and here you can see it is the left hand.

3. *Sweep the ball*   The ball must be swept from the floor, standing up and winding up in order to make the pass slows down the whole movement. (Figs 11 and 14.)

PIVOT PASS

This is a method which is used when the scrum-half needs to pass to a player who is behind him. If a scrum-half goes to pick up the ball and in doing so he is facing away from the outside-half he will need to turn towards him in order to pass the ball. He "pivots" on his front foot hence "pivot" pass.

Key factors
   1. Front foot close to ball
   2. Pivot on the front foot
   3. Wide base
   4. Sweep the ball away

Nothing of these factors need further explanation because they have been covered when describing the straight pass.

DIVE PASS

There was a time when there was a big controversy—"to dive or not to dive"—that was the question. The sensible approach is that scrum-halves in particular need to be able to do both standing and dive passes. The dive pass is always necessary when passing off a narrow base or with the weight on the front foot. In this case the scrum-half chasing the ball which is rolling quickly away from him will almost invariably have to dive pass. (Fig. 15.)

Key factor
   Leg drive—this is the only key factor as long as we bear in mind some of those mentioned in the straight and pivot passes. It is essential to drive hard with the legs in order to get impetus behind the pass and sufficient height to clear the ground for a good arm swing. (Figs 16 and 17.)

Fig. 15. This pass has to be a dive pass, because the passer is working off a very narrow base.

Fig. 16. He must drive hard with the legs in order to make space for his arms to swing.

Fig. 17. The pass completed. Perhaps it is slightly too far in front of the receiver but it is a good fault because it is making him run on to the ball.

There are two other techniques which come under handling —picking up the ball and falling on it. The inclusion of the latter under handling may surprise you but it really is a handling technique as it is a means of regaining possession.

PICKING UP THE BALL
This is a technique which all players should practise as they may be called upon to perform it many times in a game.

Key factors
   1. Approach
   2. Bend the knees
   3. Pick-up

1. *Approach* You should approach alongside the ball because then there is much less chance of falling over your own feet or indeed kicking the ball—I have seen it happen many times! (Fig. 18.)

2. *Bend the knees* Most important and probably the reason why most players fail to pick up the ball cleanly is because they fail to get down to it. (Fig. 18.)

3. *Pick-up* The fingers need to be wide spread and aiming to get underneath the ball. Having picked up the ball either distribute it or drive forward. If challenged by an opponent drive in and screen the ball. (Fig. 19.)

FALLING ON THE BALL
This is the classic way of stopping a group of opponents who are dribbling the ball or of checking a ball which is rolling away and being chased by the opposition.

Key factors
   1. Drive
   2. Get up
   3. Feed or screen

Fig. 18. When picking up the ball, approach alongside it and bend the knees.

Fig. 19. Take a good grip on the ball and drive forward. This is a good position.

Fig. 20. Drive in at the ball.

Fig. 21. Try to grasp the ball as you go down.

Fig. 22. Having landed and got firm possession of the ball, get up immediately.

1. *Drive*   Drive in to the ball with your back to the opposition, be sure to grasp the ball as you go down. (Figs 20, 21 and 22.)

2. *Get up*   The law says that no player may lie on the ball. Therefore it is important not only to practise falling but also getting up immediately with the ball.

3. *Feed or screen*   The player who gets up with the ball must be alive to what is happening around him. He must look for support and either feed or screen the ball.

5 RUNNING

There are really three kinds of running skill in Rugby football. First, we have the running skill of the ball-carrier,
secondly the running skill of the supporter and thirdly the
running skill of the defender. This chapter is mainly concerned with the running skills which can be developed in
order to beat an opponent but a word or two about running
in support and defence would not be amiss.

SUPPORT

There is a need to run intelligently in support of the ball-
carrier. If everyone rushes to the ball it could be that players
would be hindering one another and even falling over each
other. Players must try to "read" what is happening and then
make decisions accordingly. It is, for example, quite possible
to support too close and in doing so to over-run the ball
should a mistake occur. It is also very easy to support too
flat and I have often seen four or five players in a line who,
when a tackle was made, were not in a position to take part
in the game immediately because they had over-run the ball-
carrier and the ball. There must therefore be depth in support. I suppose the key factor in support running is "anticipation", trying to reason out what is going to happen.

DEFENCE

Anticipation is just as important in running in defence.
Years ago it was the done thing for forwards to "corner-flag"
so that when they left a scrum or line-out or indeed when-
ever they were covering in defence they ran towards the

corner-flag. On many occasions I have seen eight forwards following this advice and they were all running *away* from the ball. I, myself, taught "corner-flagging" for a time but, when I realised that it was a false concept, I became a bitter opponent of this kind of game. The object of running in defence is really to deny the opposition the time and the space in which to develop their attack. In other words defenders must put attackers under "pressure"; one of our principles of team play—remember? This is done by taking the game to the opposition. Again, however, it is of no use to have three or four players running at one defender if by doing so other attackers are left free. This is where the matter of anticipation is so important, trying to read what is happening and, even more important, what is going to happen.

The real options in running, however, lie with the ball-carrier; his job is to evade the defender. There are several ways in which this can be done but first the object of the ball-carrier should be to run with conviction so that he can dominate the defender. Far, too often, players carrying the ball fail to run with authority and they often get manoeuvred into positions by the defender from which there is no escape. Players, therefore, ought to have plenty of practice at running with the ball so that the ball is in no way a hindrance but in a sense is part and parcel of the player. As far as evasion techniques are concerned many players will develop their own, some indeed are unique to particular players and sometimes attempts to copy them meet with no success.

There are, however, only four ways of getting past a defender, to run inside him; to run outside him; to run through him (!) and persuading him to move out of the way, on reflection, I suppose a fifth way would be to jump over the defender. I have never seen it done but I understand that some players have done it—I would not recommend it for any but the bravest! The four ways I have mentioned can be achieved as follows; inside, with a side-step; outside, with a swerve; through him, with a hand-off and persuasion with a dummy. Let us take them one by one.

SIDE-STEP

This is the easiest of the evasive techniques to do. The most advantageous position for the ball-carrier is when the defender is coming across at right angles to the ball-carrier's path. In this situation, assuming that the defender is coming from the left, the ball-carrier pushes his right leg into the ground thus checking his speed and, by thrusting vigorously to the left, changing direction. The result will be a stepping inside the defender who will find it difficult to readjust his approach. The side-step can be executed at anything from 2 to 7 yards from the defender. It depends largely on the running speed. The faster the speed the further away the side-step can be done.

Key factors
    1. Leg drive
    2. Getaway

1. *Leg drive* This is vital if the side-step is to stand any chance of success. In order to side-step to the left, the right leg must be used as a prop with which first to check forward speed and then to drive hard to the left. It is interesting to note that in New Zealand the side-step is referred to as the "prop". One other point about the driving leg is that it can only work efficiently if the body weight is over the leg. Therefore in the instance quoted above it would be an advantage to lean slightly to the right to ensure that the weight was over the right leg when it begins to check and drive. (Figs 23 and 24.)

2. *Getaway* Although the side-step is easy to achieve it is also easy to counter. This is because when the ball-carrier moves inside he is moving nearer to the covering defence.

Fig. 23. Here is an example of how a side-step will beat a defender on the inside. The attacker has seen the inside gap and it is so obvious that the defender will be quite unable to stop him.

Fig. 24. Another side-step seen from the rear this time. I suppose ideally the attacker could have driven harder with his right leg but he has done enough to beat the defender.

He must therefore place great emphasis on accelerating after the side-step—it inevitably slows a player down—and if possible swinging back on to his original running line.

SWERVE

The swerve is achieved by the attacker deceiving the defender into thinking he is going to run inside him and then, when the defender checks to counter this, the ball-carrier accelerates past him on the outside. There is no doubt that the swerve can be most effective because it is an outside break and is therefore taking the attacker away from the covering defence. However, although it is effective it is quite difficult to do for, unless the ball-carrier has a good feint inside, which will cause the defender to check, there will be no room to get past him on the outside.

The mechanics of the swerve, assuming that the ball-carrier has received the ball from his left, are as follows: the ball-carrier swings his right leg over to the left as though he was going to run inside, he then swings his left leg to the right and accelerates away in a little arc. The swerve needs to be attempted 5 to 10 yards away from the defender again depending on running speed.

Key factors
1. A good feint
2. Getaway

1. *Feint*   Unless the attacker can make the defender believe he is going to run inside him then there is little chance of success. Therefore, in the instance outlined above, there must be a big swing over by the right leg. It crosses over the left leg and it is this movement which is the feint and which causes the defender to check. (Fig. 25.)

2. *Getaway*   The attacker must accelerate away from the feint otherwise the momentary advantage in making the

Fig. 25. The swerve—
you can see how the
attacker by swinging
the right leg in
towards the defender
has made him check.
Look how the defender
has responded to the
feint in.

Fig. 26. Now the
attacker swings the
left leg back over the
right and bears outside
the defender. See how
the defender has been
flat-footed.

Fig. 27. Away goes
the attacker,
accelerating on the
outside. Good points
to note are the lovely
balance and the ball in
two hands.

defender check will be lost. The left leg must now swing back over the right and running in a little arc will put the attacker just that little bit further away from the defender. (Figs 26 and 27.)

HAND-OFF

The laws allow the ball-carrier to "hand-off" a would-be tackler. However, only the hand is allowed and the palm must be open. This technique can be very effective when a strong runner is facing an indecisive tackler and it can be especially useful in helping to complete a swerve.

Key factors
    1. Ball transfer
    2. Hand-off

1. *Ball transfer*   The ball must obviously be tucked under the arm which is furthest away from the tackler. The timing of this is important, too soon will telegraph the intention and too late will not allow sufficient time to control the ball and prepare for the hand-off.

2. *Hand-off*   The handing-off arm should be bent so that it can, at the right moment, shoot out like a piston. This, of course, added to the running speed results in a vigorous shove in the tackler's chest or face, if he is coming in high or head or shoulder if he is lower. The player with the good hand-off can actually lever himself away from the tackler. (Figs 28 and 29.)

DUMMY

The dummy is the means by which the ball-carrier pretends to pass and so gets the defender to follow the ball or at least what he thought was the ball. There is a golden rule in

Fig. 28. Ouch! that's a good hand-off.

Fig. 29. Get away!

defence which says "take the man with the ball" but it is surprising how many players, even internationals, break the rule and "take the dummy".

Key factor

Conviction—the ball-carrier must convince the defender that he is going to pass. The technique is exactly that described in the basic pass except that the ball-carrier does not let the ball go.

6 TACKLING

So far I have only dealt with attacking options, i.e. the various choices players have when they have possession of the ball. But having ball possession is in normal circumstances only 50 per cent of the game. We must assume that the other side are going to have the ball too. We know from our principles of play that in this case we must put them under pressure, we must deny them time and space, we must take the game to them but, more than this, we must prevent the ball-carrier from running with the ball. In other words we must tackle him.

Tackling is largely a matter of determination but timing and technique also play their part. Determination will vary according to the make-up of each individual but it also stems from confidence. Players who, in their practice sessions, involve themselves in lots of physical contact gain in confidence, and determination, as a result, is often a by-product. Timing, too, needs to be developed through realistic practice but technique can be readily understood here and now by everyone. Remember, however, that understanding in the sense that you know what should happen is one thing but applying this knowledge effectively in the game is quite another.

There are one or two basic principles in relation to tackling that we ought to appreciate before we look in detail at tackling technique. We can get some useful pointers if we go back to the chapter on running. We know, for instance, that the side-step is the easiest way to beat a man. We also know that the most difficult place to beat a man is on the outside. Finally we know that going in high to the tackle or indecisively lays one open to the hand-off. In defence, there-fore, these are the factors to be taken into consideration.

The result is that when running in defence and faced with an attacker with the ball we should place ourselves inside the ball-carrier and therefore close the inside gap. This will have the effect of making him run outside and we know that it will be difficult for him to get by us here. It only remains for the defender to go low and decisively into the tackle thus avoid-ing the hand-off or "fend" as they say in New Zealand.

Having said this there are really three kinds of tackle, from the side, from the front and from the rear.

SIDE TACKLE

This is the easiest tackle to perform and every defender, if he can, aims to tackle his opponent from the side.

Key factors
1. Body position
2. Drive
3. Arms

1. *Body position* A low body position is a strong position and will enable the tackler to get under any attempted hand-off. The tackler should be aiming his shoulder for the area just above the knee. His head should be positioned behind the thigh for obvious reasons.

2. *Drive* The low body position must be combined with a powerful drive from the legs. This will result in the attacker being knocked down rather than being dragged down. (Fig. 30.)

3. *Arms* These must be used to grip the legs tightly. This action will ensure, even if the drive was not quite hard enough, that the ball-carrier will come down to the ground. Using the arms in this way means, too, that the legs are

Fig. 30. A good side tackle—slightly high but the force of the tackle has knocked the ball-carrier sideways—look at his face!

Fig. 31. Another side tackle slightly lower than in Fig. 30. Good use of the arms.

pinned and there is no chance of the tackler being kicked by a "loose" leg. (Fig. 31.)

FRONT TACKLE

Possibly the most difficult tackle, especially against the strong runner with high knees! However, sound technique helps a great deal.

The aim in all tackles is to try to knock down the ball-carrier. In a tackle from the front when the ball-carrier is almost stationary this is relatively easy. The tackler just drives straight in, waist high, aiming to knock him backwards. It is difficult to recommend this technique when the ball-carrier is running hard towards the defender. It is something to do with the irresistible force and the immovable object! Here the tackler must be more prudent and use the momentum of the ball-carrier in order to effect the tackle. Let us look, then, at a tackle on the ball-carrier running straight at the defender.

Key factors

   1. Body position
   2. Drive
   3. Arms

1. *Body position*   This is again low but the tackler aims to take the attacker at thigh-level on one shoulder. He lets the attacker come into him. He is almost in a crouching position and the momentum of the attacker takes him on to his back. (Fig. 32.)

2. *Drive*   The drive is just as explosive as in the other tackles but the timing is different. The drive in the front tackle is very late and comes at the point of impact between attacker and defender.

3. *Arms*   Must be used vigorously in conjunction with drive. They also can be used to twist the attacker so that the

Fig. 32. When faced with a player running at him from the front, the tackler tries to get him on one shoulder and "goes" with the ball-carrier.

Fig. 33. As the tackler hit the ground he tries to turn the ball-carrier so that he lands on top and can quickly take part in the game again.

defender lands on top and is thus in a good position to get back into the game quickly. (Fig. 33.)

REAR TACKLE

It is difficult in this tackle to "knock-down" the ball-carrier because he is usually running away from the tackler. The "knock-down" effect can only be achieved if the speed of the defender is greater than that of the ball-carrier. Therefore the defender aims to "drag" down the ball-carrier.

Key factors
   1. Drive
   2. Arms

1. *Drive*   In fact it is drive and dive. The defender must accelerate by driving in order to put himself in contact with the ball-carrier. This really necessitates a dive. The tackler aims slightly to one side so that he avoids falling on legs and boots.

2. *Arms*   They make contact just below the hips and the tackler lets them slide down the legs, eventually pinning the feet. It is important to grip tightly so that there is no chance of the ball-carrier running through the tackle. (Figs 34 and 35.)

SMOTHER TACKLE

This is the name given to the tackle when the defender not only stops the attacker but prevents him from passing the ball as well. Obviously the smother tackle is a bonus but there is a danger that young players will place greater emphasis on smothering the ball than on tackling the player. Stopping the player is the first priority, stopping the ball becomes a second priority. Don't forget it!

Fig. 34. In the rear tackle allow the arms to slide down the ball-carrier's leg and . . .

Fig. 35. . . . hang on!

7 KICKING

Many people lay great stress on the phrase "Rugby is a handling game" and so it is, but Rugby is also a kicking game. There was a time, some years ago, when it seemed that the ball was kicked far more than it was passed. In recent years the balance has been corrected but it is a fact that kicking plays a very important part in the game. It is an option in attack, it is a means of obtaining relief in defence and it can gain points through kicks at goal.

We must therefore give it some consideration. Unfortunately for some players kicking is just a way of opting-out. Perhaps it would be better to pass, or try to beat a man or even take a tackle, but the kick is an easy way of shelving responsibility. When the kicking is done well it can be extremely effective but, more often than not, it is done badly. Kicking, to be effective, therefore needs a lot of practice. The trouble is that the bad kick is not as apparent as the bad pass. The latter is easily seen and the man who made the mistake is exposed to all. If however he kicked the ball badly the result is not always so obvious. If it is kicked far enough by the time it lands the kicker is often forgotten! So kicking can be the easy way out.

The object, when kicking in attack, and here I must say that it ought to be one of the last options tried because it means losing ball possession, is to put the ball into an effective area. This means that when the ball lands the minimum requirement is that the kicking side should be able to challenge the opposition should they field the ball. Ideally, of course, one would like the kicking side regaining possession without having to contest it with their opponents.

As far as kicking in defence is concerned sometimes a defender is under so much pressure that he and his side are grateful if the ball is merely kicked out of play thereby stopping the game and giving them a chance to reorganise. Not all defensive kicks, however, need put the ball out of play. Kicking direct to touch in open play, as you know, can only take place from behind your own 25-yard line. Strictly speaking that is not true, you can kick to touch from anywhere, but if it is from in front of your own 25-yard line you cannot gain any ground. In this case the ball has to be brought into play opposite where it was kicked. It may, therefore, be an advantage not to put the ball out-of-play but, by kicking deep to the opposition twenty-five, give them the responsibility of making the decision. If the ball is kicked to touch, then you have the advantage of bringing it back into play. If they try to run it from the twenty-five they may find themselves in trouble unless their support is exceptionally good. However, these decisions can only be made by the player on the field, but unless you begin to think in these terms off the field then there is less chance of it happening on the field.

As far as techniques are concerned there are only four basic kicks: punt, grub-kick, place-kick and drop-kick. The first two are tactical kicks and the latter two are either kicks for points or a means of restarting the game. There are, of course, numerous variations and personal interpretations which individual players add to the basic technique but these are developed through experience and practice. I only propose to deal with the basic technique. Before I do I want to emphasise one key factor which is common to all kicks. I will not repeat it again but it is of great importance and it is that the kicker must keep his eyes on the ball until after it has been kicked.

PUNT

In the Laws under Definitions it states "A punt is made by letting the ball fall from the hand (or hands) and kicking it before it touches the ground."

Key factors
1. Handhold
2. Release
3. Kicking foot
4. Follow-through

1. *Handhold* Hold the ball at the angle which it should land on the foot. Point the ball towards the direction you want it to go. If you are kicking with the right foot it is easier to hold the ball with the left hand in advance of the right. (Fig. 36.)

2. *Release* If you hold the ball at the angle which it should land on the foot obviously the release of the ball must be such that the angle is not altered. The hands really should just move sideways to allow the ball to drop. Do not in any circumstances throw the ball up in the air. This is one reason why your hands should not be underneath the ball as this encourages throwing up in the air. (Fig. 37.)

3. *Kicking foot* The foot when it hits the ball should be stretched absolutely tight—achieved by pointing the toe. This provides a rigid platform with which to hit the ball. Bad kicking is more often than not the result of a "loose" foot. Pointing the toe very slightly inwards also helps. The outside lace holes of the boot make contact with the ball. This means that the ball is struck with the instep not the toe. (Fig. 38.)

4. *Follow-through* This is the result of correct kicking technique and not something which you try to do afterwards. If you kick through the ball you will get a good follow-through.

Fig. 36. The punt—hold the ball in the way it should land on the foot.

Fig. 37. Drop the ball so that it lands on th foot in precisely the same way that it w being held. Excellent technique—notice th angle of the ball and eyes on the ball.

Fig. 38. Kick through the ball with a stretche foot. This is beautiful technique.

GRUB-KICK

Even though the Rugby ball is oval in shape it is possible to exercise great control over it. The grub-kick is one where the ball is kicked into the ground and rolls along the ground. Very useful if you need to put the ball in touch from in front of your own 25-yard line or can be used to push the ball through defending players who are coming up fast and flat.

Key factors
  1. Handhold
  2. Release
  3. Kicking leg
  4. Follow-through

1. *Handhold*   The ball must be held so that the seam is pointing absolutely straight along the line of intended direction. This kind of accuracy is essential in order to get full control over the ball.

2. *Release*   Again the ball must be released so that it maintains the same "line" as when it was being held.

3. *Kicking leg*   The ball is kicked forward into the ground. Aim to get the knee over the top of the ball—this will keep it low. The ankle once again should be stretched to provide a good kicking "pad". If the ball is struck correctly it will roll end over end in a straight line and this helps those following it up.

4. *Follow-through*   If the ball has been kicked correctly the follow-through will result in a bent leg with a high knee.

PLACE-KICK

A kick that is used for kicks at goal and for starting and restarting the game. This latter function is often ignored but it needs to be practised otherwise a bad kick-off will result in giving possession to the opposition.

There are two techniques normally used in the place-kick. One is the toe-kick where the kicker lines everything up in a straight line, i.e. posts, ball, run-up and hits the ball with his toe, following through in a straight line. It is often regarded as the classical method. The other technique is where the ball is hit with the in-step (the inside of the foot) and the kicker approaches the ball in an arc, hence the name of "around the corner kicking" which it is sometimes given. Both types of kick can be very effective. The best kick for you is the one with which you can achieve the highest percentage of success!

Here, the coach trying to help a player has something of a problem, toe-kicking technique is well defined but in-step kicking is largely a matter of individual adaptation and when something is going wrong it is difficult to decide what it is as there is no basic technique which the coach can use as a guide. I will content myself with describing the technique of the toe-kicker. If you are a successful in-step kicker—stick to it! On the other hand, if you are not getting success try the toe kick.

Key factors
1. Ball placement
2. Run-up
3. Non-kicking foot
4. Kicking foot
5. Follow-through

1. *Ball placement*   However the ball is placed, either upright or pointing forwards, (probably better), it must be "teed up". It is a mistake to dig a hole in the ground and then push the ball into it. You are trying to get the ball in the air, therefore make a tee which will give it a start.

2. *Run-up*   The approach to the ball should be controlled with a smooth acceleration. The last stride to the ball must

be a long one so that the kicking leg is left a long way behind. It can then be accelerated through to hit the ball hard. A short last stride nearly always results in a "stab" kick.

3. *Non-kicking foot*   All sorts of arguments have raged as to where the non-kicking foot should be in relation to the ball. Take it from me the non-kicking foot should land behind the ball not alongside. Your job is to get the ball in the air. You want to hit the ball when your foot is swinging upwards. If you put your foot alongside, then the kicking leg will still be moving downwards.

4. *Kicking foot*   The ankle is rigid but this time at right angles to the lower leg and not with the toe stretched. (Fig. 41.)

5. *Follow-through*   A long last stride and a kicking leg which is pulled through to hit the ball hard will result in a good follow-through. "Kicking through the ball" is what you should think about.

DROP-KICK

This form of kick is still worth 3 points when it is done in open play and it is a relatively easy method of scoring. It also has to be used to restart the game either at the centre or at the 25-yard line. For this reason alone it needs practice.

The actual kick itself is achieved by dropping the ball on to the ground and kicking it as soon as it rises.

Key factors
   1. Handhold
   2. Release
   3. Kicking foot
   4. Follow-through

Fig. 39. Holding the ball for a drop-kick. It is tilted slightly backwards.

Fig. 40. Follow-through after a drop-kick. Th result of good kicking. Look at the stretche foot.

Fig. 41. The place kick—this is the "toe-kick technique. Compare the position of the foc here with those in Figs 38 and 40.

1. *Handhold*   The ball must be held in the position which you want it to land. This means that it must be leaning slightly backwards. (Fig. 39.)

2. *Release*   It must be released so that the angle at which it was held in the hands is maintained.

3. *Kicking foot*   The toe should be stretched to give a rigid ankle.

4. *Follow-through*   Again the result of good kicking technique. (Fig. 40.)

8 DEVELOPING SKILL

The preceding chapters have dealt with the techniques of basic individual skills but, as I pointed out earlier, learning the technique is not necessarily the same as learning the skill. Technique is merely the way to perform a movement, skill is applying that technique in the game. For instance, the basic pass is a means of getting the ball from A to B. It is possible to become very good at doing just that, getting the ball from A to B in a situation where there is no opposition and where there is plenty of time to do it. In other words, no pressure. Learning to pass well in those circumstances does not automatically mean that you will pass well in a game. This, however, is what we are trying to do and therefore we must devise practices which will develop skill. Therefore any practice must be as realistic as possible, it must be as close to the game as possible. It must involve pressure.

There are two kinds of pressure which we can achieve in practice, one is the pressure of opposition and the other is the pressure of time. We therefore should practise in competitive situations. Some people have little imagination and they often think that the only competitive situation is a full game of Rugby football. If this were the only means by which we could improve then some players would have to wait a long time for, as beginners playing in a full game, they would not touch the ball very often, if at all!

In order to get the greatest amount of practice we need to work in small areas and in small groups. It is especially useful for young players to know these kind of practices because it means that they can improve their ability at the game without having to have available twenty-nine other players and a referee.

Modern games coaching has in recent years used a coaching or training grid in order to get over certain fundamentals. Such grids are being increasingly used in Rugby football and they are excellent for beginners. A grid is a number of squares marked out on the ground. There can be any number of squares of any size, depending on how many players are required to use them.

I am now going to suggest a number of practices which are both enjoyable and purposeful as far as Rugby is concerned. Some of them only required one 10-yard square and some of them can be done in such a square marked out on a hard surface such as a gym floor or a playground.

All the practices will require one or more of the techniques previously described but most of all you should remember that the only reason we need to develop these skills is so that we are better able to:

1. Go forward
2. Support
3. Keep the ball moving (continuity)
4. Pressurise the opposition when they have the ball

These are the principles of team play.

1. Team passing

Work in a group of three in a 10-yard square. Count the consecutive number of passes you can make before you drop the ball. Aim to put the ball in the perfect place for the receiver. You must pass on the run and move in all parts of the square. Those not in possession of the ball should aim to support the ball-carrier. Work off the ball. A development is to count number of passes in thirty seconds.

2. Team passing—two or more groups

Two or more groups of three working independently in one square. As in 1 above, the aim is to count the consecutive number of passes either before the ball is dropped or in a given period of time. Players now have to make decisions because, although there is no opposition, there are a lot of players working in a confined space. This means that players not only have to learn to give passes but sometimes to withhold them because another player may be in the way. It is a very elementary way of learning *when* to pass. The aim again is continuity and support in a mild pressure situation.

3. Two against one (Pig in the middle)

Three players in one square. Two players with the ball interpass and count consecutive passes. The third player opposes them (no contact whatsoever) and tries to intercept the ball. If he succeeds or the ball is dropped he changes place with the player responsible. Work to a maximum time limit of one minute. Aim is continuity and support with the opponent learning how to apply pressure.

4. Three against three (or two against two)

Six players in one square. Three players with the ball are opposed by the remaining three. Count consecutive passes or see if the ball can be retained for a specific period of time—one minute. Opponents (non-contact) try to intercept the ball and to put pressure on the players in possession. An interception or dropped ball means that the sides change over. Again continuity and support coupled with pressure situations are the aim.

5. Three against three (contact)

The development of activity number 4 is to allow the opposition to make contact with the ball-carrier. The conditions therefore are as in 4 with the exception of the opposition being allowed to tackle the ball-carrier in a *standing* position. Neither ball-carrier nor tackler are allowed to fall to the ground. The job of the ball-carrier is now to keep the ball available for the support. This is a skill which has to be learnt. Just as important, too, is the ability to "rip" the ball in these close contact situations.

This is best done by getting the whole arm in between the ball and the ball-carrier's body and then, by using the shoulder to punch down, to twist away from the ball-carrier. If it is done vigorously there is little chance of the ball-carrier being able to retain possession.

The aim is still continuity and support but now the pressure has become more intense.

6. Three-man Rugby

Three players oppose three others in two 10-yard squares, i.e. 20 yards by 10 yards. Aim is to score a try. Forward passes are not allowed. Standing tackles only. We are now working on all the principles of team play—going forwards, supporting the ball, keeping it moving and pressurising the opposition.

Next development would be to allow tackling to the ground.

7. Support drill

Six players using five 10-yard squares, i.e. 50 yards by 10 yards. Number the players 1–6. Number 1 with the ball starts to run down the 10-yard corridor, Number 2 calls "Two" and is given the ball. Number 3 shouts and so on. The ball must not go outside the corridor and the time taken to score a try 50 yards away is recorded. Aim is then to beat it. If there are twelve players, then a race between two teams can take place either with or without timing.

8. Support drill (variation)

Details as in 7 but this time the ball-carrier calls out a number—any number. For instance Number 1 with the ball may call out "Five". Number 5 would then have to come up to take the pass. It works very well as long as the ball-carrier does not shout out his own number!

9. Line passing

Three players using one square. Three players with a ball stand on a line and run to another line 10 yards away inter-passing the ball. As soon as they reach the line they turn quickly and run back turning each time they reach the line. Count the number of passes in a specific period of time, say twenty seconds. It is quite feasible for good handlers to get in more passes than there are seconds. In other words, in twenty seconds I would expect good handlers to make at least twenty-five passes. The middle man tends to get the best practice and players should inter-change for subsequent attempts. Any forward passes are not counted.

10. Support line passing

Three players to run 50 yards. Three players line up with the ball held by Number 1 standing on the right. He starts to run and passes to Number 2 on his left who passes to Number 3. Number 1 in the meantime has run behind Number 2 and come up outside 3 who gives him the ball. Number 2 does the same thing and so on. The danger in this activity is that the movement goes across field instead of forward. It is therefore important for players to run straight and especially for the last man in the line to allow the man coming behind and outside him to straighten up before he gives him the ball.

11. Two versus one

Three players using two squares, i.e. 20 yards by 10 yards. Two players with the ball stand on one line. The defender stands on the other line 20 yards away. The aim is for the attackers to score a try. The defender tries to stop them either by two-handed touch or by tackling. Number 1 has three attempts as the ball-carrier, then as the supporter then as the defender. The others move around in the same kind of way. Count the scores in the various positions.

12. Three versus two

Five players in two squares, i.e. 20 yards by 10 yards. A development of number 11. This time there are three attackers and two defenders. It is also possible to work in four squares, i.e. 20 yards by 20 yards. This however makes the "pitch" rather wide and can encourage cross-field running.

13. Picking-up support drill

Six players in five squares, i.e. 50 yards by 10 yards. Six players line up one behind the other. Number 1 with ball runs two or three strides and places ball on floor, Number 2 follows picks up and does likewise. Meanwhile Number 1 goes to the back of the team and so on. Either time it or have a race against another team.

14. Screen pass support drill

Six players in five squares, i.e. 50 yards by 10 yards. Six players line up one behind the other. Number 1 with the ball runs three strides, slows down, drops one shoulder and pushes the ball back in both hands to the opposite hip. Number 2 accelerating comes in low and takes the ball, he then slows down and screens the ball for Number 3. Meanwhile Number 1 has gone to the back of the team. Time or race.

15. Picking-up and screening support drill

A combination of 13 and 14. Six players using five squares, i.e. 50 yards by 10 yards. Number 1 with the ball runs two or three strides places the ball on the ground. Number 2 picks up and screens the ball for Number 3 who after running two or three strides places it on floor, Number 4 picks up, screens and so on.

16. Screen pass drill

Six players, two tackle-bags, one square. Two players rest; two players, one behind each tackle-bag standing on two lines 10 yards apart. Two players, one with ball. Ball-carrier runs and drives into bag, screening the ball. Supporter takes ball from him and both players run around the bag and drive at the other bag and so on. Each player does five screen passes. As the last pass is made the runners take a rest, the resters hold the bags and the bag-holders become the runners. Aim to get thirty passes in two minutes.

17. Tackle-bag drill

Six players, two squares, i.e. 20 yards by 10 yards. Use three lines 10 yards apart. Players line up one behind the other, tackle-bag standing on middle line. Number 1 tackles bag, runs to far line, touches it and runs to pick up bag. He then goes on to touch Number 2 who runs to tackle bag and so on. Count number of tackles in two minutes.

If the bag will not stand up by itself, Number 1 starts off holding the bag and Number 2 runs to tackle. Number 1 goes to back of team. Number 3 runs as soon as Number 2 picks up bag.

18. Tackling drill

Six players, one square. One player against five. Count the number of tackles made in thirty seconds, then change the tackler. Hand-offs not allowed. Players must not run outside the square.

19. Dribbling and falling football

Six players, two squares, i.e. 20 yards by 10 yards. Three players try to dribble the ball over opposing three players' goal-line. Opponents may only stop the dribble by falling on the ball. As soon as they fall on the ball they must get up and try to dribble over their opponents' goal-line.

20. Punting Tennis

Six players, five squares, i.e. 50 yards by 10 yards. Three players working in two of the end squares oppose three players in the two other end squares. The centre square is no-man's-land for players and the ball. One player standing in an end square punts the ball into the opposition squares. If they catch it they may kick it back. If the ball is dropped or goes out-of-bounds or a player or the ball goes into the middle square a point is lost. The serving is done alternately.

21. Drop-kick Tennis

As in 20 but with a drop-kick instead of a punt.

22. Kicking Golf

Mark out a course, e.g. first hole could be to punt from the 25-yard line over the crossbar; second hole could be to hit a corner post; third hold could be to grub kick under crossbar and between posts and so on. Get a partner, one ball each, count number of kicks required to complete course.

All the above activities are meaningful as far as the game is concerned. They are the means by which skill can be developed. Most of them, too, make great demands on fitness. Players therefore need a certain basic fitness level before they can practise. Practice will not only make players more skilful but it will also improve the particular fitness requirements of the game. You must however remember one thing in this respect the fitter you are the longer you can practise and the longer you practise the better you become at the game. Someone said once that the only place where success comes before work is in the dictionary. This was never more true than in the case of Rugby Football.

9 MINI-RUGBY

(a) DETAILS OF THE GAME

Having learnt a new range of skills we now need a form of game in which we can express them. Many people would think immediately of the 15-a-side Rugby game. This would not be my choice. I firmly believe that the 15-a-side game is too complicated for beginners, irrespective of their age. The range of skills required for the full game together with the laws involved make too many demands on those who are new to the game. The result is nearly always depressing to watch—thirty players chasing the ball; little involvement—so few players touch the ball and consequently there are few opportunities for players to acquire and develop the fundamentals of the game.

The alternative, of course, is to play a modified game of Rugby with reduced numbers and less requirement in terms of skill and law. The Welsh Rugby Union has recently devised such a game and I am happy to say that I played a part in designing it. The game is called "Mini-Rugby". It is intended especially for boys in the Primary School, i.e. those under twelve years of age but, of course, it is eminently suitable for beginners of any age. I think I should make it clear that Mini-Rugby is not intended in any way to replace the full 15-a-side game. It could not possibly do this, but it is an excellent "lead-up" to the big game. As there are standards and rules laid down for Mini-Rugby it means that as well as being an introductory game it can also be played competitively. This is a great advantage, most introductory games get forgotten in the haste to progress to playing the big game and the result is that the skills and principles which can be developed through a modified game are often neglected.

In Mini-Rugby the emphasis is on handling, running and contact. These are the main elements of Rugby Union football and those who see the mini-game played can have no doubt as to what kind of game it is. There is another quite important factor, too, and that is that small schools are not denied the opportunity of playing Rugby because they do not have a sufficient number of boys. The game can be fitted to their own particular circumstances, in fact Mini-Rugby can be played with any number from seven to twelve players.

Perhaps it would be helpful if I were to give some further details of Mini-Rugby and show how it differs from the full game. We know that the game is called "Mini-Rugby" and that it can be played with as few as seven players or as many as twelve. I think nine is ideal and four of these should be forwards and five backs. I want to look a little closer at these players.

Forwards

There are four forwards and if you are astute you will wonder how they can pack down in a scrum. The answer is by putting two players in the front row and two in the second row. Of the second row players, one would be a lock and the other a flanker who must always pack on the same side on which the ball is being put into the scrum.

Backs

The backs would comprise a scrum-half, an outside-half, one centre, one wing and a full-back. I prefer having a wing and a full-back rather than two wings. The reason here is that the full-back is a key man in modern attacking back play and he cannot be exposed to this concept too soon. Although I mention one centre and one wing I would probably get them to switch according to which side play was developing. For instance on the left-hand side of the field the left wing would be just this but on the right-hand side he would become the centre and the centre would now be the right wing. This, of course, is an ideal situation I am well aware that this must be tailored according to the capabilities of the players.

Variations

The above formation applies to the 9-a-side game. Other formations are as follows:

(*a*) 7-a-side—3 forwards—2 in the front row
                4 backs—scrum half, outhalf, centre, wing
(*b*) 8-a-side—3 forwards—2 in the front row
                5 backs—as in 9-a-side
(*c*) 10-a-side—5 forwards—two in the front row
                5 backs—as in 9-a-side
(*d*) 11-a-side—5 forwards—two in the front row
                6 backs—as in 9-a-side but two wings
(*e*) 12-a-side—5 forwards—two in the front row
                7 backs—as in 15-a-side

Playing pitch

It is quite ludicrous to see small boys trying to play the game on a pitch which was designed with men in mind. Therefore with reduced numbers there is an even stronger case for a smaller pitch.

The dimensions of a Mini-Rugby pitch should be 75 yards long by 40 yards wide. (Fig. 42.) In my view this is ample in size for a 9-a-side game. In fact the size was chosen after a lot of deliberation because it approximates to the area on a full-size pitch which is bounded by the half-way line, the 25-yard line and both touch-lines; the game being played across the pitch. If the game is played on a full-size senior pitch, then this is the area which should be used. (Fig. 43.) Yes, I know the pitch is only 30 yards wide and that it is on

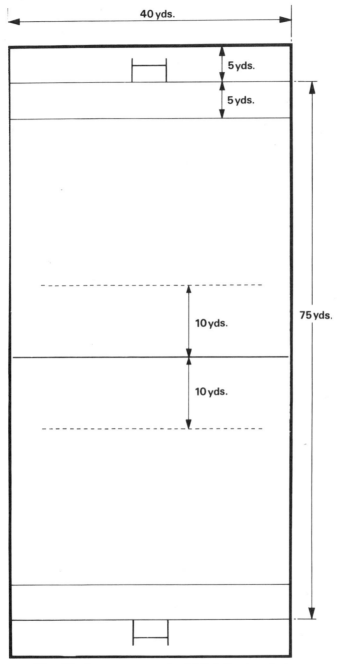

Fig. 42. A purpose-marked Mini-Rugby pitch.

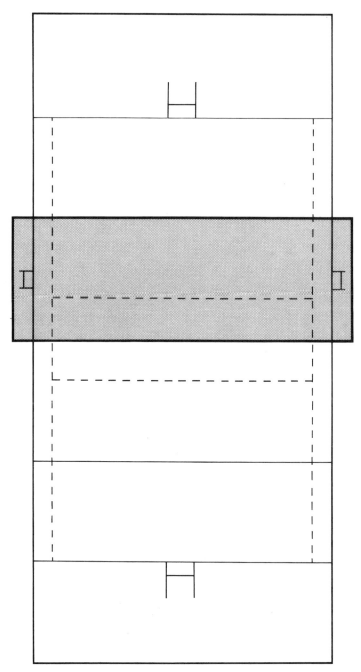

Fig. 43. A Mini-Rugby pitch marked out on a senior pitch.

the narrow side but at least it encourages players to go forward and to attack the goal-line and not the touch-line.

Some may suggest using half a pitch but this is still too big and especially too wide which encourages cross-field running. There is, too, always the hazard that when players run parallel to the goal-posts as opposed to running towards them they might collide with them.

As many mini-games will take place on a full-size pitch and as it is not practical to put down additional markings we must make use of those lines already there. This means that all drop-outs will take place from behind a broken line drawn 5 yards from the goal-line. This is utilising the 5-yard line on a full-size pitch. We do not have a half-way line unless it is a purpose-marked Mini-Rugby pitch—a small pile of sand or sawdust as a centre spot will provide a sufficient guide.

The dead-ball lines are a maximum of 5 yards from the goal-lines.

Goal-posts

These again should be reduced in size, goal-posts 15 feet apart and crossbar $8\frac{1}{2}$ feet high. On a full-size pitch portable posts can be used, otherwise the senior posts are utilised for conversion kicks which are always taken from 20 yards in front of the posts irrespective of where the try is scored.

Fig. 44 shows the dimensions of the goal-posts and an idea, using angle brackets, of how to make the posts portable. They are secured to the ground by means of earth-pins. These must be covered with a sand-bag in order to eliminate the injury risk.

Kicking

Some teachers will not allow their players to kick the ball when they are in the early learning stage and it is not a bad idea. However, players need to develop the full range of individual skills in order that they can exercise judgement

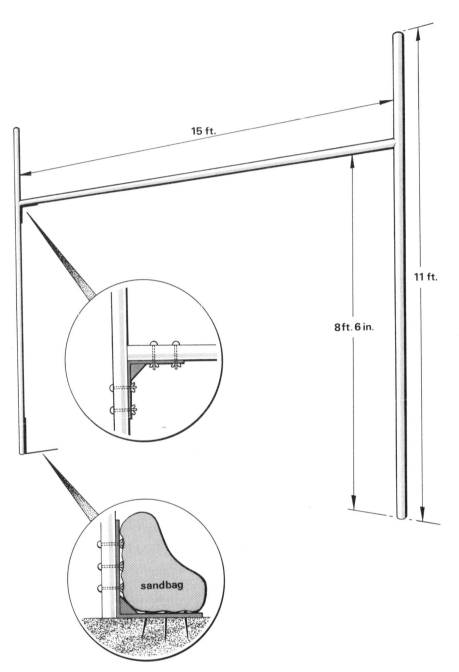

15 ft.

11 ft.

8 ft. 6 in.

sandbag

Fig. 44. Mini goal-posts, the inset diagrams show methods of fixing.

therefore kicking is allowed in the mini-game. However it should not be encouraged at the expense of other skills, therefore direct kicking to touch is not allowed unless it is a penalty kick or a kick from within the 5-yard area.

Penalty kicks at goal are not allowed and all conversion kicks after a try are taken from in front of the posts.

Touch

When the ball goes into touch the game is restarted by a scrum 10 yards in from the touch-line. This means that there are no lines-out in Mini-Rugby and this alone makes the game both in skill and in law that much easier.

Duration of play

The duration of the game can be varied to suit the age of the players but with eleven-year-olds two halves each of fifteen minutes is about right.

(b) MINI-SCRUM

I would prefer young players to regard the mini-scrum as merely the means by which the ball can be brought into play. Those who know me well might be surprised to see this kind of statement from me because I have long been an advocate of the importance of the scrummage. In the 15-a-side game I regard the scrummage as the supreme platform on which everything else depends. However, it is because I know that young players around the age of twelve years have neither the physical strength nor the mental maturity to scrummage in this way that I do not emphasise the role of the scrum in Mini-Rugby. My view is that any teacher or coach who expects young players to scrummage like senior players would be guilty of an error of judgement. Players of this age want to get hold of the ball and to run with it. I am concerned with giving them that opportunity.

As I mentioned earlier the mini-scrum in the 9-a-side

game has four players from each side. Two players form the front row and there are two in the back row. This method of having two players in the front row is much easier than having a front row of three. It is not revolutionary because New Zealand, until the law changed in the 1920s, always packed two in their front row. They regarded a two-man front row as being highly efficient. Some people feel that we should retain the three-man front row in Mini-Rugby because it is a requirement of the big game. I do not accept this view, I am looking for the easiest method of getting the ball into play via some sort of scrum and there will be plenty of opportunity for players to learn the skills of the three-man front row at a later stage.

On occasions teachers have come to me complaining that the combination of the two-man front row together with the two-man back row makes an unbalanced unit and there is some truth in this. However, we have four forwards and we have to put them in some kind of formation. A three-man front row in a four-man scrum would be much worse. A five-man scrum with two in the front row causes no problem. Let us get back to our four-man scrum. The first thing we must do is realise that it is not sufficient just to take away a prop forward from a three-man front row and then assume that we have got two players suitable for a two-man front row—we have not.

Almost inevitably we would have a prop forward, usually a biggish boy, and a hooker, usually much smaller. It is quite unrealistic to expect these two players to scrummage effectively. In producing the four-man scrum we must get two players in the front row who are reasonably well-balanced in size and who are as big and strong as they can be at this age. This is important because they have both to resist and transmit shove. The smaller players can act as the Number 8 and the flanker. One other point is that there will always be a tendency for any scrum to wheel to the loose-head side, i.e.

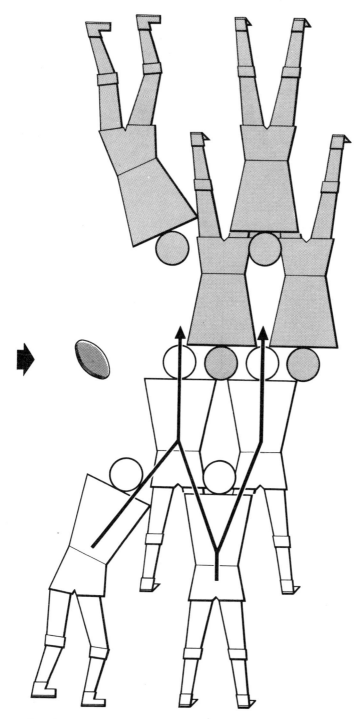

Fig. 45. A mini-scrum with four forwards on each side. The arrows show the direction of shove.

to the left. Therefore it should be stressed to forwards that it is their responsibility to keep the scrum square to the front. (Fig. 45.)

The key factors in scrummaging are:

1. Foot positioning
2. Snap Shove
3. Mechanics

1. Foot positioning

The feet must be placed in such a way so that not only will there be a channel down which the ball can come when it is hooked but players will also be able to push forward.

The loose-head prop, who packs on the left, should pack with his feet apart although he can have his left foot slightly in front of his right. In this way he will be solidly placed and because his legs are apart this will make a channel for the ball.

The tight-head prop, on the right, will also act as hooker. He should strike for the ball with his right foot. The law allows him to strike with either foot but the far foot gives much more control over the ball. His left foot should be back so that as well as striking with his right foot he can push with his left leg. When hooking for the ball which the opposition are putting in it is necessary to strike with the near foot because of the distance from the ball.

The Number 8 forward packs between the props and he must get his legs back. He will do better if he pushes off the inside of his feet.

The flanker, who must pack on the same side of the scrum on which the ball is being put in, should pack with his feet back but his inside leg can be in advance of his outside leg.

The ball channel is between the flanker and the Number 8. This is Channel 1; as players get more experienced and when circumstances demand it, e.g. a slow ball or a slow

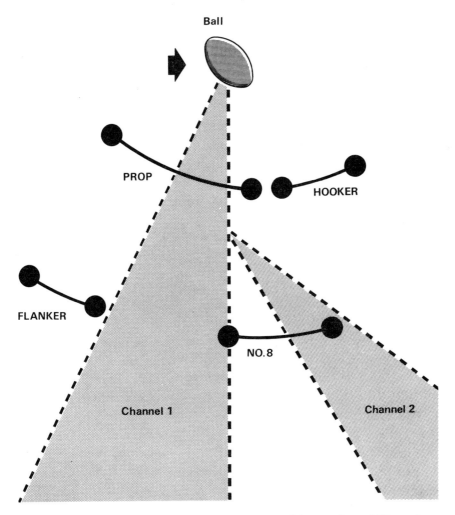

Fig. 46. This diagram shows the foot placing of forwards and illustrates the two ball channels.

scrum-half who is always getting caught, it will be an advantage to put the ball on the right-hand side of the Number 8. This is Channel 2. (Fig. 46.)

2. Snap Shove

The hooking of the ball is made a little easier if the scrum moves forward as the ball is being struck. This means that forwards must push hard as the ball is put into the scrum. Obviously it is more effective if it is done by the four players in the scrum acting as one rather than separately and much more so if, as well as being together, the four men drive dynamically rather than push slowly. This is what we call "Snap Shove" and two points will help. First you cannot shove off straight legs therefore knees must be bent, and secondly, getting players to shout "now" as the ball goes in has a dramatic effect.

3. Mechanics

The first point to mention is that players must grip as tightly as they can. This will help to consolidate the scrum and will probably stop it from disintegrating. Both props must try and stay square and resistant to the front. This is slightly more difficult for the prop who is going to hook. Incidentally I do recommend that props should always pack on the same side, so that in a sense they are both hookers, one on the tight-head and one on the loose-head.

The Number 8 shoves straight forward with perhaps slightly more emphasis on shoving to support the prop who is hooking. This will help counter-act the wheel to the loose-head.

The flanker packs out at a slight angle and tries to push the prop inwards and forwards. (Fig. 45.)

Finally there are two other essential requirements if forwards are to be able to shove effectively. One is that they must have straight or flat backs. This is best achieved by forcing the head upwards. Secondly they must have their shoulders in the correct place. This applies to the Number 8 and flanker. Their shoulders must be under the buttocks of the props. A good tip when getting down is to kneel on one knee and to place the shoulder just above the knee of the prop. As you lift your own knee off the ground you slide the shoulder up the thigh, when it reaches the right shoving spot it will stop. This is nature's niche designed for forwards to shove against!

(c) MINI-MAUL AND MINI-RUCK

There are two further skills which we will need in Mini-Rugby and these are mauling and rucking. As we have a game with reduced numbers so we will have mauls and rucks with reduced numbers. Remember, too, that the ability to maul and ruck is not something which only forwards should be able to do. Often a back may find himself in a situation where he must set up a maul or ruck in order to protect possession.

Before I discuss the techniques involved it is important that we know what constitutes a maul and what constitutes a ruck. The essential difference is that in a maul the ball is held in the hands while in a ruck the ball is on the ground. Therefore a maul consists of one or more players from *each* team closing around a player *carrying* the ball and a ruck consists of one or more players from *each* team in physical contact and closing around the ball which is in *on* the ground between them. Incidentally a maul and a ruck can only take place in the field-of-play, i.e. the area bounded by the touch-lines and the goal-lines.

The key factors in mauling and rucking are precisely the same although the techniques do differ. My contention, for some time, has been that the maul is more important than the ruck because the ball in the hands is easier to control than the ball on the floor. Therefore we should be looking for mauls and not rucks.

Key factors (Maul and Ruck)

1. Firstest with the mostest
2. Body position
3. Drive
4. Ball not the whistle

1. *Firstest*   We must get more people to the maul or ruck before the opposition do. The reason is obvious.

2. *Body position*   The maul or ruck start 5 yards from the ball and players coming in must come in low, leaning from the hips. This is a strong position.

3. *Drive*   When they reach the ball they must keep driving forward and MUST stay on their feet.

4. *Ball*   If the referee blows his whistle, then those players in the maul or ruck have failed.

Let us now look at the particular techniques required

Maul

The key man is the ball-carrier, he must try to drive through tackles using his shoulder and slipping the ball back. If he is checked before he can get rid of the ball he sets up a maul. He does it by turning his back on the opposition. He then bends low at the hips and his back makes a platform for the supporting players. The first two players bind in over the top of the back of the ball-carrier. They drive forward and parallel to the touch-line. They aim to keep the ball-carrier on his feet and keep the ball channel clear. The next player coming in (and we will not get more than four players in a mini-maul) goes in for the ball and stays tight in the maul. He can then feed the ball at his discretion.

Ruck

A ruck takes place when the ball is on the ground there-fore players must come in a low body position so that they can hit the ruck with their shoulders. They should grab a team-mate as they come in low, hard and parallel to the touch-lines. They must aim to drive beyond the ball; they must bind tight and drive hard. They should try to walk over the ball without touching it but, if they are checked, the ball should be raked back with the feet.

(d) TACTICAL CONSIDERATIONS

Before we can begin to discuss the tactics of Rugby football we must first understand what is meant by gain and tackle lines. The gain line is a very simple concept. It is that line which runs parallel to the goal-lines through the centre of the scrum, maul or ruck. Until you have crossed that line with the ball you have made no gain of any description. The tackle line is just as simple. It is the line on which the defending team meets the attacking team in order to effect the tackle. The gain line is a static line in each situation but the tackle line moves according to the speed of the attack and defence. For instance a very quick defensive line of players coming up to the tackle will move the tackle line nearer the attacking team. There is a close relationship between gain and tackle lines which must be appreciated in order to understand the tactical situation.

The implications of gain and tackle lines will be more clearly understood by reference to the accompanying diagrams. In Fig. 47 it can be clearly seen that at the scrum the half-way line is also the gain line. Crossing this line is a key factor for effective team play. "Go forward" is a principle of play—remember? However, there is a tackle line to contend with as well and this very often produces problems. The tackle line, as we know from above is that line on which opposing players meet. In Fig. 47, because the opposing players are the same distance from the gain line, the gain and tackle lines coincide. It is a situation which we often refer to as stalemate. However, more explosive running on

Gain & Tackle Lines

Fig. 47. Gain and tackle lines causing stalemate.

the part of the attacking team will allow them to cross the gain line before they meet the tackle line. This must always be a principal aim.

However, it must be remembered that defending teams are not usually as free with space as the defending team in Fig. 47. Putting pressure on the opposition when they have the ball is another principle of play therefore the defenders tend to get as near to the gain line as they can taking off-side laws into consideration. In Fig. 48 we see exactly this situation. The defending Black team will cross the gain line long before the White attackers can reach it. In these circumstances the tackle line is said to be superior. If Whites run and pass in this situation they will be ineffective unless in some way they break the tackle line or force it backwards. Any tackle successfully made will allow Blacks to run forward to the tackled ball, and Whites, on the other hand, although they have won possession, but used it ineffectively, will be unable to go forward.

What then are the implications of gain and tackle lines? Perhaps this can best be illustrated in Fig. 49. In Situation A it would appear that Whites are not well placed to attack because of their position in the field. However, if we look at this situation closely and analyse it we will see that the opportunity for attack is very favourable. Blacks, because they have a territorial advantage, have lined up deeply. If White can produce "good ball" they can obviously cross the gain line long before Blacks can. This means that even if a White player is tackled, his side will be going forward. This is certainly an advantageous position.

In Situation B Whites would appear to be well placed for a running and handling back line movement. However, on closer analysis it can be seen that they will have to break the tackle line before they can cross the gain line. In these circumstances they would be well advised to try something other than an orthodox back-line attack.

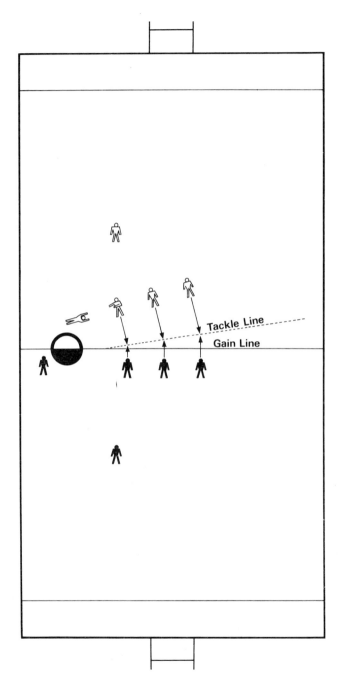

Fig. 48. Tackle line superior.

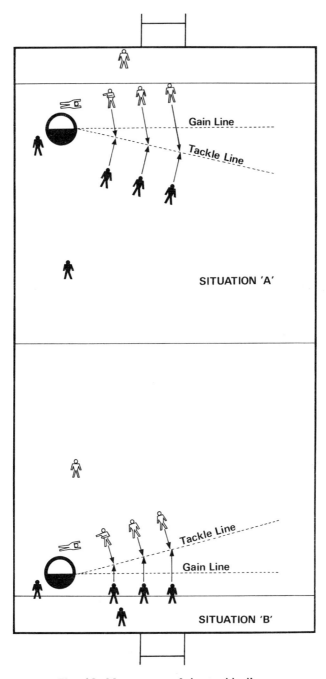

Fig. 49. Movement of the tackle line.

In conclusion one must say that all players whether backs or forwards must realise the implications of gain and tackle lines. We should not allow it to dominate our thinking otherwise we will produce a robot-like reaction from players, but we must be aware of our situation in the field and of the possibilities both for attack and defence. Some may say that this is too complex for young boys to grasp. I, for my part, would hope that this chapter and its accompanying diagrams make the issue crystal-clear!

(e) POSITIONAL RESPONSIBILITIES

We have, I think, built up a fund of information on how to play Mini-Rugby and so equip players with some of the background skill and knowledge which is necessary in order to play the 15-a-side game well. For instance, we know how the game is organised; we know something of individual technique and skill; scrum, maul and ruck in relation to Mini-Rugby have been clarified and we should be aware of the implications of gain and tackle lines. It would therefore appear that we know all that is required—not quite.

So far I have not mentioned anything about the positional functions of players. These must be appreciated if we are to produce a good team performance. I do not want to deal with individuals I think it is easier and simpler if we look at units. I want therefore to talk in terms of ball-getters, linkers and strikers.

(i) Ball-getters

The forwards are the ball-getters. Their first job is to obtain possession and to feed it back correctly. In Rugby we often talk about "quality possession" or "good ball". This is precisely what the ball-getters must try to achieve. There is nothing more embarrassing or painful to a scrum-half than to receive a ball to which are attached several members of the opposition! This was how the term "hospital-pass" originated. Possession of this kind is very definitely bad ball and must be avoided if at all possible.

As far as Mini-Rugby is concerned the ball-getters must work hard on improving the skills required in scrum, maul and ruck. Good technique in these aspects of play will allow other members of the team the necessary time and space to develop an attack.

However, forwards must not think that ball-getting is their only job. It is their first job, once they have done this and fed it back correctly then they must remember the principles of going forward, support and continuity. They must therefore try to get in positions which will enable them to do this.

(ii) Linkers

The linkers are the half-backs, i.e. scrum-half and outside half. Their first job is to act as links between the ball-getters and strikers. It is very important for young players in particular, to understand this, otherwise we will get a lot of individual and selfish play. The scrum-half must try to get the ball away from scrum, maul and ruck as quickly and as smoothly as possible. The outside-half must try to run on to the scrum-half's pass. This will enable him to get his line of three-quarters moving forward, so that they will stand a chance of playing the game in front of the gain line.

Half-backs must not think that they should not make breaks, of course they should, if the opportunity is there. These, however, should be a variation of play rather than something to be attempted every time a half-back has possession of the ball.

As with ball-getters, once the linkers have parted with the ball they must work to get involved in the game again.

(iii) Strikers

The strikers are the centre, wing and full-back. Their first job is to get across the gain line. Once this is achieved they

will be going forward and making it so much easier for
other players to support them. If the continuity skills are
good, then in these circumstances it is very difficult for any
side not to play well.

Strikers, however, must realise that there are many ways
of crossing the gain line. They should not think that the
responsibility belongs to them alone. If this were the case we
would have players tucking the ball under one arm and
completely ignoring both their own side and the opposition.
Strikers should endeavour to penetrate by strong explosive
running but at the same time they must "read" the situation.
They must be aware both of the opposition and the support.

The concept of ball-getters, linkers and strikers is a very
elementary one. It gives each unit a primary function or a
first objective. Once this has been achieved it is the function
of *all* players to support attacks in whatever way they can.
The roles in a sense are interchangeable. For instance a
scrum-half may be tackled in such a way that he forms a
maul; he now is a ball-getter. A forward might, in these
circumstances, have to become the scrum-half and therefore
he is a linker.

If players can be encouraged to think in these terms then
Mini-Rugby will make a great contribution to the 15-a-side
game because players brought up in this way will be well-
versed in the fundamentals of running, handling and contact
skills. They will know the value of support play; how to use
space; how to co-operate with others. What a marvellous
background on which to build the more complicated unit
skills required both by forwards and backs in the 15-a-side
game.

Near the beginning of this book I said that I did not want you to be too concerned with the laws of the game. For a start there are twenty-seven of them and quite a number are really for the information of the referee. Some laws are absolutely straightforward but others require a little explanation because they are often misunderstood. I think it would help if we looked at a few of the latter as they apply in Mini-Rugby.

Advantage

I want to begin first with an unwritten law, it is not in the law-book but it is probably the most important law of all. It is—"play to the whistle". Do not stop because you think the whistle should go. The referee may be applying the greatest law in Rugby football, the advantage law. This means that if one side commits an offence the referee does not automatically blow his whistle because it could be that the non-offending side have gained an advantage and obviously they should be allowed to exploit it. Advantage can be tactical or territorial. By tactical we usually mean a good attacking opportunity, e.g. a player knocks-on the ball and the opposition obtain possession with perhaps two or three of their players opposing one or two. If, on the other hand, after the knock-on, the opposition kicked the ball ahead and chased it, this would be territorial advantage. Remember then, play to the whistle.

Try

The object of the game is to score tries and therefore it is important that we should know how to do it. You score a try by grounding the ball in your opponent's in-goal area. "Grounding" means, while holding the ball in one or both hands, placing it on the ground or, if the ball is already on the ground, placing hand(s) or arm(s) on it and pressing downwards or, while the ball is on the ground, falling on it so that the ball is anywhere under the front of your body from waist to neck.

Tackle

The definition of a tackle is very explicit and a number of conditions apply. A tackle can only take place in the field-of-play, i.e. the area bounded by the touch-lines and the goal-lines, you must also be held in such a way so that, for a moment, you cannot pass the ball or the ball touches the ground. These three conditions must apply at the same time—you must be held in the field-of-play and you must either be unable to play the ball or the ball must touch the ground. You can see that it is perfectly possible to be brought to the ground but if the ball does not touch the ground you can pass it because you are not tackled. You should understand that there is no law against passing off the ground; the law is against playing the ball after a tackle. One other thing, remember you do not have to be brought to the ground in order to be tackled. You can be held while standing on your feet but if you cannot play the ball then you are tackled.

Remember if you are tackled you must immediately release the ball, and, if you are on the ground, you must get away from it.

Knock-on

I think everyone knows that in Rugby you are not allowed to knock or throw the ball forward. "Forward" means in the direction of your opponents' dead-ball line.

The "knock-on" law has recently been altered and now it can be regarded in the same way as a cricket catch. This means that if you go to catch the ball in your hands direct from a pass or kick and, having failed to take it cleanly, if you can recover it before it touches the ground or another player it is not a knock-on.

There is one exception to this and that is, if you charge down a kick and the ball goes forward from your hands it is not a knock-on even if it does touch the ground. It must have been a charge-down however and not an attempt to catch the ball.

Lying on the ball

Earlier in the book I mentioned the technique required for falling on the ball. This is a perfectly legitimate movement but having fallen on the ball you are not allowed to stay there. You must either play the ball in some way or roll away from it.

In-goal

Many people think that the in-goal area is a no-man's-land where the laws do not apply. This is not so. All the laws apply in the in-goal area. What may appear to be exceptions are not really so. A player cannot be tackled in the in-goal area because a tackle can only take place in the field-of-play. This means that any player carrying the ball in the in-goal area who was collared by the opposition, would not have to release the ball because a tackle as defined in law, cannot take place in the in-goal area. The same applies to scrum, ruck and maul. They can only take place in the field-of-play.

Any offence by the attacking side in the in-goal area results in a twenty-five drop-out while an offence by the defending side results in a 5-yard scrum with the attackers putting in the ball.

Off-side

This law causes the greatest amount of misunderstanding so let us deal with those aspects which apply to Mini-Rugby.

Open play

By open play I mean other than scrums, mauls and rucks.
You are off-side in open play if you are in front of a player
on your *own* side who has the ball or was last to play it. This
does not mean that the referee will blow his whistle and
award a penalty against you. If this were the case the game
would never get going because all players will sometimes,
during a game, be in front of a player on their own side who
has the ball. Being off-side means literally "off the side" and
until you are put on-side you cannot take part in the game. If
you are off-side and try to take part in the game, then the
referee will almost certainly blow his whistle and award a
penalty kick against you.

If you happen to be off-side and within 10 yards of a
player *waiting* to receive the ball, you must immediately
retire until you are 10 yards away. It is not sufficient to
stand still, your very presence will have an effect on the
player waiting to receive the ball, therefore you are interfer-
ing in play. Get 10 yards away at once.

Obviously if you are off-side you must know what you
can do so that you can take part in the game again. There are
two ways you can be put on-side; one way is by the action of
your own team, the other way is by the action of the opposition.

Your own team can put you on-side, even if you are
within 10 yards of an opponent waiting to receive the ball,
provided you are *retiring*, when

(1) the last player on your side to play the ball has moved
in front of you or you behind him, or
(2) one of your team carrying the ball has run in front of
you, or
(3) one of your team, who was behind the last man on
your side who played the ball has moved in front of
you.

The opposition can put you on-side when

(1) an opponent carrying the ball has run 5 yards, or
(2) an opponent kicks or passes the ball, or
(3) an opponent *intentionally* touches the ball but does not catch it.

It is important to understand that if you are within 10 yards of an opponent waiting to play the ball, you cannot be put on-side by any action of your opponents. You must get 10 yards away at once.

Scrum

Off-side at scrummage can be clearly understood if you imagine that there is a line drawn parallel to the goal-lines through the last foot at the rear of each pack of forwards. This gives us two parallel lines—like tram-lines—which extend from one touch-line to the other. While the ball is in the scrum any player, unless he is the scrum-half or part of the scrum, who goes into this area is immediately off-side. The lines are called "scrummage off-side lines" and all players must stay behind their own scrummage off-side line until the ball is out of the scrum.

The exceptions to this law are the scrum-half, but even he must stay behind the ball, and players binding in the scrum. Provided he is behind the ball, a player in the scrum may leave it as long as he retires *immediately* behind his own scrummage off-side line.

Maul and Ruck

Off-side at maul and ruck are precisely the same. The off-side lines are the same as those for the scrum, i.e. through the last foot at the rear of each group of players. This time, however, there is no dispensation for anyone to be in front of the maul or ruck off-side line. Any player in front of the off-side line must either join the maul or ruck, behind the ball, or retire behind the off-side line immediately. Failure to do so means that the player is off-side and the referee will almost certainly award a penalty kick against him.

These, then, are some of the laws which cause most problems. The best advice I can give is play to the whistle and accept the referee's decisions without question. Once he has given a decision he cannot alter it, unless a touch judge had previously indicated that the ball was in touch. If you are puzzled by a decision you can always at the end of a game approach the referee politely and ask him for clarification. This is perhaps the best way of learning the laws.

11 TESTING YOUR SKILL

A recent development in many sports has been the establishment of Award Schemes. In the objective sports like athletics, swimming, weight-lifting, etc., it is very easy to devise tests which will give a real indication of a competitor's ability. In team games, however, it is much more difficult because purposeful practice essentially means working with others against opposition. It is difficult in these circumstances to measure a player's ability because he is dependent on the ability of his team-mates and also on the quality of the opposition.

Award Schemes, however, properly used are very valuable for they provide an incentive for players to practise. They act as a yardstick by which players can measure improvement and progress. The question is whether any such tests can be devised for Rugby bearing in mind what I said earlier about the problems involved in measuring game's ability. I think that such tests can be devised provided they are carefully thought-out and properly conducted. I have appended some Rugby "tests" below. One point in their favour is that the individual player can practise on his own and the tests are such that there is a real possibility that excellence in the tests will transfer to the game situation.

It is hoped that the Welsh Rugby Union will, in fact, use these tests as a basis for Achievement Awards for players under 12 years of age.

The tests are as follows:

Test 1

    Equipment: Three lines 10 yards apart; 1 ball (size 3), 1 stop-watch.

Test: Stand on starting line; ball on the centre line. Run, pick up ball—score a try on the far line. Still carrying ball, turn around run back to centre line, place ball, run back to touch ground beyond starting line and repeat. Record the total time taken.

Test 2

Equipment: A 10-yard square marked out on ground, in the centre is a 5-gallon oil drum (weighted so that it cannot be knocked over) standing on a box 2 feet high. Four balls (size 3), each one placed 2 feet outside the corner of the square, 1 stop-watch.

Test: Player stands at one corner outside the square and when given the word picks up the ball and does a standing pass aiming to hit the oil drum. One foot only be allowed to be in the square. As soon as he has passed he runs to the next corner and so on until he finishes on the original starting point. Count the number of hits and record the total time.

Test 3

Equipment: A 10-yard square marked out on ground. Four touch flags—one in each corner. In the centre is a 5-gallon oil drum (weighted so that it cannot be knocked over) standing on a box 2 feet high. Four balls (size 3) one in each corner, 1 stop-watch.

Test: Starting from one corner pick up the ball and run to another corner: while running pass the ball to hit oil drum. Forward passes do not count and player must not run into the square. Run around the square until original starting point is reached. Repeat, running in the opposite direction. Record hits and total time taken.

Test 4

Equipment: Four chairs placed at 5, 10, 15 and 20 yards. One ball (size 3); 1 stop-watch; starting line.

Test: From the starting line run forward dodging in between the chairs, run around the end chair and return
dodging between the chairs, score a try over the starting line. Ball must always be carried in two hands
except in the actual movement of scoring the try when
grounding with one hand is permissible. Record the
time taken.

Test 5

Equipment: Restraining line (goal-line), touch-line, 25-
yard line and 5-yard line (as on pitch). One ball (size
3).

Test: Stand behind restraining line at least 15 yards from
touch line. Kick ball to touch. Three attempts with right
foot to left-hand touch and three to right-hand touch
with left foot. Score as follows:

(*a*) Ball *direct* to touch nearside of 25-yard line, 1
point.
(*b*) Ball *direct* to touch far-side of 25-yard line, 3
points.
(*c*) Ball pitches in 5-yard area far-side of 25-yard
line and then goes into touch, 4 points.

Test 6

Equipment: Target 2 feet square (either nailed on post or
painted on wall); bottom of target 6 feet from ground.
Three lines marked 5 yards, 7 yards and 9 yards from
the target. One ball (size 3).

Test: Throw the ball over-arm (right or left) to hit target.
Two attempts from each line. Score 1 point for a hit.

Test 7

Equipment: A line drawn on a hard surface, e.g. playground or wooden floor.

Test: Standing Broad Jump. Stand with both feet behind
line and with a two-footed take-off jump as far as pos-

sible to land on two feet. Measure and record the best of three attempts.

Test 8

   Equipment: 1 set regulation senior goal-posts. One ball (size 3).

   Test: From 20 yards in front of the posts, using either foot—2 place kicks, 2 drops kicks, 2 punts to kick ball over crossbar between uprights.

   Three points for a goal.

   Two points for a hit on crossbar or uprights above bar.

   One point for a hit on upright below bar.

   Record total points.

Once a player has established his own standards, he can be retested at intervals and can measure his improvement accordingly.

There is one real danger in tests of this kind and that is that more time can be spent on testing individuals than on learning to play the game. This is a factor which must be borne in mind. Provided this is taken into account I believe that these kinds of tests have a useful contribution to make towards acquiring certain specific skills.

12 TESTING YOUR KNOWLEDGE

How well do you know your Rugby football or how well have you read this book? This chapter consists of a series of questions. How many can you get right? I have deliberately omitted giving a long list of answers, that is a soft option. The answers are all in the text of this book and if you do not know an answer you must go back and do some more reading.

Question 1

Name the boy who is credited with inventing Rugby football?

Question 2

In what year did he do his famous deed?

Question 3

Wales beat the 1905 All Blacks—what was the score?

Question 4

Name the All Black who said that he scored in this match?

Question 5

In what year was the Rugby Football Union formed?

Question 6

Give the correct name for the supreme governing body in Rugby Union Football

Question 7

How many laws are there in Rugby football?

Question 8

What is Law 7 called?

Question 9

What are the four principles of team play?

Question 10

If "technique" is "how" what is "skill"?

Question 11

What is the first key factor when running with the ball?

Question 12

When is "tucking" permissible?

Question 13

When should you try to take a ball from a pass?

Question 14

Give two reasons why, when taking the ball from a kick, you should try to turn slightly to one side

Question 15

Give two reasons why you should emphasise swinging the ball when passing?

Question 16

Where should you be aiming to pass the ball?

Question 17

What is the purpose of the screen pass?

Question 18

What should the supporter taking a screen pass emphasise?

Question 19

In executing a switch pass what is the first thing the ball-carrier should do?

Question 20

What is the big advantage the spin pass has for a scrum-half?

Question 21

How should you hold the ball for a spin pass?

Question 22

When do scrum-halves have to dive pass?

Question 23

What is the most important factor in trying to pick up the ball?

Question 24

Having fallen on the ball what should you do?

Question 25

In supporting the ball what should the supporters be trying to do?

Question 26

Where is the easiest place to beat a defender?

Question 27

Why is the successful swerve very effective?

Question 28

What is the key factor for a successful swerve?

Question 29

Where should the ball be for a hand-off?

Question 30

"Tackling is largely a matter of . . ."?

Question 31

What is regarded as the easiest tackle to make?

Question 32

Where should the tackler's head be in a side tackle?

Question 33

Why in all tackles should you use the arms?

Question 34

In a tackle from the front what should the tackler try to do as he hits the ground?

Question 35

Name the key factor common to all kicks

Question 36

"Bad kicking is more often than not the result of . . .?"

Question 37

When should you use a grub-kick?

Question 38

In a place-kick where should the toe-kicker put his non-kicking foot?

Question 39

How can you ensure a good follow-through?

Question 40

When holding the ball for a punt you are advised not to have your hands underneath. Why?

13 PERSONAL

We have read a lot about principles of play, techniques, skills and means of developing them but, expert though we may be at these things, if our personal attitudes towards the game are wrong then our success will only be temporary.

Rugby football has survived for well over a hundred years and become one of the World's greatest amateur sports as much by the spirit it creates as by the skill with which it is played. In this modern age it is often "clever" to sneer at terms like the "spirit of the game" and "ethics" but Rugby football, in company with other sports, has demonstrated on many occasions that these qualities are not entirely lost. Of course there have been instances when the halo has slipped temporarily but these have only emphasised what a precious heritage we possess. It is our responsibility, those of us who play and coach the game, to preserve and enrich it. We must ensure by our actions, both on and off the field, that we do nothing to discredit the game.

One of the features of Rugby football is that it is a game of physical contact and it is inevitable that hard knocks will be given and taken. It is vital that these take place within the context of the game. Any player taking part in this kind of physical contest knows that there is an injury risk even though the ethics and the laws may be strictly observed. He should never be subjected to risks which are outside both ethics and law.

In essence we must respect the game and those who take part in it. We must especially respect the authority of the referee. His judgement and decision must be final, accepted without hesitation and certainly without question.

Presumably we play the game because we enjoy it, that is probably the best reason. But let us remember that there is no disgrace in wanting to be successful; there is no dishonour in wanting to win. All players should pursue excellence, each, according to his ability, will achieve varying degrees of success. We cannot all be internationals but we can all display high standards of behaviour and sportsmanship. Defeat must be accepted with good grace and victory with humility.

Perhaps, however, all I am trying to say can be summed up so much better, and in far fewer words, by quoting from the Object of the Game which is part of the Laws of Rugby Union Football. It says the Object of the Game is that two teams "observing fair play according to the Laws and a sporting spirit, should by carrying, passing and kicking the ball, score as many points as possible, the team scoring the greater number of points to be the winner of the match".

GOOD LUCK and *GOOD RUGBY*